WORKBO

DISCOVERING
DANIEL

AMIR TSARFATI
& DR. RICK YOHN

HARVEST PROPHECY
AN IMPRINT OF HARVEST HOUSE PUBLISHERS

Cover design by Faceout Studio, Molly von Borstel

Interior design by KUHN Design Group

For bulk, special sales, or ministry purchases, please call 1-800-547-8979.
Email: CustomerService@hhpbooks.com

Discovering Daniel Workbook
Copyright © 2024 by Amir Tsarfati & Rick Yohn
Published by Harvest House Publishers
Eugene, Oregon 97408
www.harvesthousepublishers.com

ISBN 978-0-7369-8840-7 (pbk)
ISBN 978-0-7369-8841-4 (eBook)

Printed in the United States of America

24 25 26 27 28 29 30 31 32 / BP / 10 9 8 7 6 5 4 3 2 1

CONTENTS

HOW TO USE
THIS WORKBOOK

What should you look for when you open your Bible? How do you draw out the meaning from what you are reading? And how do you make it work in your life?

Over the years of teaching people how to study the Scriptures, we have refined the process and will be using the following fourfold approach to the book of Daniel as spelled out in this chart.

EXPLORE THE BIBLE YOURSELF

1. CAPTURE THE SCENE (What do I see?)

2. ANALYZE THE MESSAGE (What does it mean?)

3. COMPARE THIS CHAPTER WITH THE REST OF SCRIPTURE (How is it supported elsewhere in the Bible?)

4. EXECUTE (How does this affect my life?)

CAPTURE THE SCENE (What do I see?)

This is the observation stage. As you read the Scriptures, you want to examine the passage with a series of questions, including, What am I seeing? What am I feeling? Who is speaking? Who are the main characters in the passage? What is he (or are they) saying? Why is he saying what he is saying? When is this situation taking place? Where is it occurring?

ANALYZE THE MESSAGE (What does it mean?)

At this stage, you want to dig a bit deeper and see what you can learn from the passage. What teaching is present here? What instructions am I being given? What is the intent of this passage?

COMPARE THIS PASSAGE WITH THE REST OF SCRIPTURE (How is it supported elsewhere in the Bible?)

Our understanding of God's Word is always enhanced when we look to the surrounding context or parallel passages. There is much to gain when we examine comparable stories or teachings in Scripture.

EXECUTE (How does this affect my life?)

This is the application stage. Once we let the passage speak for itself and understand it, we're ready to search for any life lessons that might be present in it. At this point, we ask, What can I learn about God or Christ? What doctrine or principle is taught here? And how can I take these lessons to heart so they influence how I think and live?

With these guidelines in place, let us now begin our study of Daniel!

SETTING THE STANDARD

DANIEL 1

G od had been exceedingly patient.

Some 120 years earlier, judgment came down upon the northern kingdom of Israel. Prophet after prophet had warned the people to turn from their wickedness. But they didn't listen. With brutal force, the armies of Assyria descended upon the northern kingdom, and took the Hebrews captive into exile and slavery.

And now, the southern kingdom of Judah faced a similar fate. Judgment was looming. The prophets had been ignored. The people had repeatedly spurned God. At last, the Lord said, "Enough!"

Among the Jewish people, Daniel was a rare exception. He was one of the few who had remained loyal to God. He also understood the threat posed by the Babylonian armies. He knew they were ruthless and took pity on no one, whether a baby, a mother in distress, an old man, or a woman—none mattered. He knew that what the Assyrians had done to the northern kingdom, the Babylonians would do to the southern. They would destroy the city of Jerusalem and the temple. And they would pillage everything of value, taking these treasures back to Babylon along with the captives.

Daniel was among those taken into exile. He and his fellow Hebrews lost everything. But King Nebuchadnezzar and his soldiers could never take away Daniel's love and commitment to the Lord. This young Hebrew had a relationship with God that was unusual among other men of his generation.

Growing up, Daniel most likely had been trained in the Torah and other writings of Scripture. This would include the book of Jeremiah, which would come in handy many years later. He was also aware of God's many promises to Israel, and he knew his people's history.

Though Daniel's heart was broken by what he saw in the chaos surrounding him, he accepted that God must have allowed this to happen. He may have wondered why God did not intervene and stop the horrible onslaught carried out by King Nebuchadnezzar. After all, as the prophet Habakkuk had said, the Babylonians were "a bitter and hasty nation which marches through the breadth of the earth, to possess dwelling places that are not theirs. They are terrible and dreadful" (Habakkuk 1:6-7).

But Daniel left that matter up to God.

One "possession" Daniel could take with him to his foreign home was the memory of those who came before him—men of God who had persevered through great difficulty without compromise. He would have heard of Job, whose life was turned upside down by Satan, yet he did not curse God. Though Job's friends and even his wife rebuked him, Job was steadfast. In the end, God honored Job by giving him twice as much as he had before everything was taken away.

Daniel would also have known about Noah, who found grace in the eyes of the Lord because he was a man of righteousness living in a degenerate world. On a planet that had never seen rain, Noah set about building a large boat. This surely puzzled his onlookers. But Noah's obedience ended up saving him, his wife, his sons, and their wives. Though water literally destroyed Noah's world, God gave him and his family a new beginning.

Then there was Joseph, who was hated and rejected by his brothers and sold into slavery. After being falsely accused by his master's wife, he was thrown into prison. There, he interpreted the dreams of two fellow prisoners, who quickly forgot what he had done for them. But later, he was called upon to help interpret dreams that had bothered the Pharaoh. And God honored Joseph by making him the number two ruler in Egypt.

Though Nebuchadnezzar could take away the familiar, comfortable, and beautiful amenities of Jerusalem—a great city set on a hill—he could never take away what counted the most in the heart of this young man we know as Daniel.

Daniel and some of his friends were forcibly removed from their homes and surroundings to live in a faraway city filled with spiritual darkness, depravity, and demonic worship. Life took the most dramatic turn possible for them.

Yet they did not let their circumstances dictate how they responded. Daniel and his friends did not respond with fear to the unknown. They trusted that God would sustain and preserve them. As we make our way through the book of Daniel, we will see this trust on display, and learn how their example can help us today.

CAPTURE THE SCENE (What do I see?)

Using your Bible, answer the following questions.

1. What did King Nebuchadnezzar and the Babylonian army do to Jerusalem and the treasures in the house of God, the temple (Daniel 1:1-2)?

2. Upon returning to Babylon, which of the Hebrew captives did Nebuchadnezzar want brought to him, and what qualifications were they expected to meet (verses 3-4)?

3. For what purpose did Nebuchadnezzar want these captives, and how long would their training period last (verses 4-5)?

4. Which four captives are named (verses 6-7)? Give their Hebrew names, and the Babylonian names assigned to them.

5. What did Daniel resolve not to do, and why (verse 8)?

6. What was the nature of the relationship between the chief of eunuchs and Daniel (verse 9)?

7. When Daniel requested that he and his friends not eat or drink of the king's food, how did the chief of eunuchs answer at first (verse 10)?

8. What test did Daniel propose, and how did the chief of eunuchs respond (verses 12-14)?

9. What was the short-term result of the test (verse 15)? And the long-term result (verse 16)?

10. Who enabled Daniel and his friends during their training period (verse 17)?

11. After all the training was completed, what did King Nebuchadnezzar find out about Daniel, Hananiah, Mishael, and Azariah (verses 18-20)?

ANALYZE THE MESSAGE (What does it say and mean?)

Using both your Bible and your copy of the book *Discovering Daniel*, answer the following questions.

1. How long of a journey was it for Daniel and the other Jewish exiles from Jerusalem to Babylon (see page 22 in *Discovering Daniel*)?

2. What do you think was Nebuchadnezzar's intent in trying to "rebrand" Daniel and his friends by giving them Babylonian names (see page 26 in *Discovering Daniel*)?

3. What is the likely reason Daniel and his friends didn't fight against being given new names (see page 28 in *Discovering Daniel*)?

4. Why did Daniel and his friends believe they shouldn't eat and drink the food provided by King Nebuchadnezzar (see page 30 in *Discovering Daniel*)?

5. Daniel and his friends showed significant and noticeable differences after only ten days on their preferred diet. What does this tell us (see pages 33-34 in *Discovering Daniel*)?

6. How else did God honor the four young men, according to Daniel 1:19-20 (see page 34 in *Discovering Daniel*)?

7. On page 35 of *Discovering Daniel*, we read, "Every decision as to whether we sin or not is a big one, because every sin is big." Why is this true?

COMPARE THIS PASSAGE WITH THE REST OF SCRIPTURE
(How is it supported elsewhere in the Bible?)

1. How does God call His people to live with regard to the world?

   a. Deuteronomy 14:2—

   b. 2 Corinthians 6:17-18—

   c. 1 Peter 2:9—

2. What does Scripture say about those who engage in compromise?

   a. James 4:4—

b. 1 John 2:15—

3. According to Hebrews 7:26, what did Moses give up when he lived a separated life?

4. What principle does Matthew 6:24 teach about compromise?

5. What questions should we ask ourselves when confronted with a choice or decision?

EXECUTE (How does this affect my life?)

1. What are some ways that we attempt to justify compromise?

2. Why is it dangerous for us to think that "small" compromises are okay? Once we've justified small compromises, what is likely to happen?

3. What consequences do you think compromise can have on your relationship with God?

4. Read Luke 16:10.

   a. What principle is taught here?

   b. In what ways did God reward Daniel for his faithfulness?

      1) Daniel 1:9—

      2) Daniel 1:15—

      3) Daniel 1:20—

5. What do you think it means to "be a vessel for honorable use, set apart as holy, useful to the master of the house, ready for every good work" (2 Timothy 2:21)?

6. In what one or two areas of your life can you improve in being "useful to the master"?

7. Read John 14:21. When we obey God, what are we showing to Him?

8. How did Daniel and his friends respond to being taken into exile and separated from their former way of life?

9. Have you ever found yourself in a difficult situation that required major changes in your life? What mistakes did you make? How could you have responded better?

CLOSING THOUGHTS

In the times when we find our world turned upside down—as happened with Daniel and his friends—we're prone to ask: Where is God when bad things happen to good people?

That question has been asked by countless people through the ages. When we are going through tough times, we may wonder, *Is God aware of my situation? If so, why doesn't He stop it and make things better?*

In the times when we doubt God is with us, it's helpful to remember what happened to Daniel and another servant of God when they found themselves in difficult circumstances.

In Daniel's case, we read that when Daniel was faced with a choice between compromise (eating the king's food) or conviction (abstaining from the king's food), "*God had brought Daniel* into the favor and goodwill of the chief of the eunuchs" (Daniel 1:9).

And back when Joseph was unjustly thrown into prison after being falsely accused of seducing Potiphar's wife, "*the* Lord *was with Joseph* and showed him mercy, and He gave him favor in the sight of the keeper of the prison" (Genesis 39:21).

In both situations, God was right there *with* His servants. Though they found themselves in tough situations, we see God at work *within* their circumstances.

So when we find ourselves asking, Where is God?, He is right there by our side. He has not gone away. We might not *feel* that He is near, but our feelings should never dictate our faith. God has promised, "I will never leave you nor forsake you" (Hebrews 13:5).

No matter what situation we face, God is faithful. He always has been, and always will be.

THE IMPOSSIBLE DREAM

DANIEL 2

Nebuchadnezzar's dream had disturbed him greatly. So much so that he was determined to get a correct interpretation of it. He sensed that a very important message was being communicated to him. And he didn't want to settle for anything less than the exact meaning of that message.

But no one in the kingdom of Babylon could interpret the king's dream. Nebuchadnezzar's wise men, magicians, and sorcerers found this an impossible task. They had hoped the king would at least share the details of his dream. That would give them a starting point for making up an interpretation that seemed plausible. But with no information in hand, they were truly left in the dark. They didn't dare take wild guesses at what the king had seen in his dream. To do so would expose them as frauds worthy of death.

Out of desperation, the wise men cried out, "There is not a man on earth who can tell the king's matter...It is a difficult thing that the king requests" (Daniel 2:10-11).

All of this was unfolding exactly as God intended. He wanted to speak directly to Nebuchadnezzar—the most powerful monarch on Earth in that day. We can be certain that it was God Himself who had inspired Nebuchadnezzar to refuse to share the details of the dream with his wise men. Behind the scenes, God was orchestrating all this to ensure that his trusted and faithful servant Daniel would get an appointment before the king.

When at last Daniel was brought before Nebuchadnezzar, he began by stating the bad news: "Your wise men are correct. There is no one who can interpret the dream. That is humanly impossible."

It wouldn't be surprising if, in that instant, the king's anger was roused. He may have thought, *Well, then, why are you here, wasting my time?*

But then Daniel followed with the good news: "There is a God in heaven who can tell you the meaning of your dream."

I can't, but God can!

That's a great way for us to view all the problems we face in life. When we find ourselves unable, we need to remember that God is able. When we are confronted with obstacles, we need to call upon the God who can overcome those obstacles. Whenever we face the impossible, we need to remember: I can't, but God can!

Then we need to pray and watch God do what He alone can do.

God is the God of the impossible. Consider the apostle Paul's evaluation of the God who sits on His throne in heaven: "Now to Him who is able to do exceedingly abundantly above all that we ask or think, according to the power that works in us, to Him be glory in the church by Christ Jesus to all generations, forever and ever. Amen" (Ephesians 3:20-21).

The first blessing to note here is that God "is able." You and I might not be able to deal with a specific situation, but He is.

The second blessing is that He is able "to do." What we cannot do, God can. More importantly, God knows exactly what needs to be done. We may think we know the best solution, but often, we don't. Perhaps God answers in a way we don't desire or expect. But we can trust that He knows what is best for us and for the situation at hand.

And the third blessing is that God can do "exceedingly abundantly above." He can do far more than we imagine or think possible.

Isn't that amazing? Our God is the God of the impossible. That was true in Daniel's day, and it's still true in ours. He can do whatever needs to be done. And when we place our full trust in His power and sovereignty, we will experience the deep inner peace that comes from knowing He is in full control. The outcome is in His hands. The best response we can have in any crisis is to trust Him.

CAPTURE THE SCENE (What do I see?)

Using your Bible, answer the following questions.

1. When King Nebuchadnezzar first asked the wise men to interpret his dream, what was their response (Daniel 2:4)?

2. What did the king say he would do if the wise men couldn't interpret the dream (verse 5)?

3. What accusation did the king make in verses 8-9?

4. When the wise men said it would be impossible to interpret the dream, how did the king react (verses 12-13)?

5. When Daniel found out about the king's decree to kill the wise men of Babylon, what did he do (verses 14-16)?

6. What did Daniel then ask his three friends to do (verses 17-18)?

7. When God revealed the details of the dream to Daniel, how did Daniel respond (verses 20-23)?

8. Before Daniel explained the dream to King Nebuchadnezzar, whom did he credit as the revealer of the dream's meaning (verse 28)?

9. Give a brief summary of what Nebuchadnezzar saw in the dream (verses 31-35).

10. What did Daniel say the dream revealed about Nebuchadnezzar himself (verses 37-38)?

11. What did Daniel say about the kingdom that would rise after Nebuchadnezzar's kingdom (verse 39)?

12. What did Daniel say about Earth's final kingdom (verse 44)?

13. What was Nebuchadnezzar's response to Daniel? And what did he say about Daniel's God (verses 46-49)?

ANALYZE THE MESSAGE (What does it say and mean?)

1. Nebuchadnezzar's wise men included magicians, astrologers, and sorcerers. Interpreting dreams and divining the future was part of their job. But what did the king do to put them to the test (see page 41 of *Discovering Daniel*)?

2. The wise men told Nebuchadnezzar they could not give the king the details and interpretation of his dream. What do you think God wanted Nebuchadnezzar to realize about his wise men?

3. When Daniel and his friends heard the troubling news that a kill order had gone out on the wise men—including them—how did they respond, and who did they turn to for help (see page 42 in *Discovering Daniel*)?

4. In Daniel's prayer in Daniel 2:20-23, what do we learn about God?

5. In his dream, Nebuchadnezzar saw a statue. What did the first kingdom—the head of gold—represent (see page 49 in *Discovering Daniel*)?

   a. What was the good news about the head of gold (see page 50)?

   b. What was the bad news (see page 50)?

6. What did the next three kingdoms represent (see page 51 in *Discovering Daniel*)?

7. What did the fifth or final kingdom represent (see page 52 in *Discovering Daniel*)?

8. Who will rule this final kingdom (see Isaiah 11:10 and page 53 in *Discovering Daniel*)?

9. How long will this final kingdom endure (see Revelation 20:4-6 and page 54 in *Discovering Daniel*)?

10. Daniel went from being on the king's kill list to being "ruler over the whole province of Babylon and chief administrator over all the wise men of Babylon" (Daniel 2:48). Why do you think God honored and protected Daniel, and put him in this position in Nebuchadnezzar's kingdom?

11. What three character traits do we see exhibited by Daniel in this account (see pages 56-57 in *Discovering Daniel*)?

COMPARE THIS PASSAGE WITH THE REST OF SCRIPTURE
(How is it supported elsewhere in the Bible?)

1. Read Genesis 41:39-41. How had the Pharaoh of Egypt responded when Joseph interpreted his dream?

2. What parallels do you see between Joseph and Daniel?

3. Nebuchadnezzar's wise men were sorcerers and astrologers. What does God say about such practices and those who do them, according to the following passages?

   a. Leviticus 19:31—

   b. Leviticus 20:6—

   c. Isaiah 44:24-25—

   d. Jeremiah 27:9-10—

4. Daniel and his friends trusted God to protect and deliver them. How do the following passages increase your confidence in God's care for His own, including you?

   a. Psalm 4:3, 8—

b. Psalm 23:4, 6—

c. Psalm 27:5, 13-14—

d. Psalm 37:15-18—

EXECUTE (How does this affect my life?)

1. Can you think of two or three other individuals in the Old or New Testaments who immediately turned to God for help in a crisis? What lessons can we learn from their examples?

2. Why do you think prayer is a vital first step when it comes to facing life's problems?

3. According to Nebuchadnezzar's dream, there will someday come a kingdom that wipes out all human kingdoms. The accomplishments of men will turn to mere dust. How should this truth shape the way we view our human accomplishments?

4. In light of the previous question, read Matthew 6:19-20. What are some ways you can grow in terms of laying up treasures in heaven?

5. Daniel was quick to give credit to God for doing what only He could do. What are some things God has done in your life that you can credit Him for?

6. Why do you think it's important for us to have a regular habit of giving God credit for all that He does for us?

7. What conclusion do you think Nebuchadnezzar would have come to if Daniel had failed to give credit to God? How do we hurt ourselves—and others—when we fail to make it clear that it's God who enables us in everything we do?

CLOSING THOUGHTS

King Nebuchadnezzar was both grateful and puzzled. He was relieved that Daniel had interpreted his dream. And he agreed with the assessment that the Babylonian kingdom was superior to all the others, as indicated by the head of gold.

But the king didn't like the fact that someday his kingdom would be replaced by another. And that eventually, still another kingdom would come that would "break in pieces and consume all these [other] kingdoms, and it shall stand forever" (Daniel 2:44).

Up until now, Nebuchadnezzar had worshipped Babylonian deities like Nabu, Marduk, and Bel. Upon hearing Daniel's interpretation of the dream, the king recognized—for the first time—a more powerful God than any other he had known. So amazed was the king that he said, "Truly your God is the God of gods, the Lord of kings" (verse 47).

All of this had to be hard for Nebuchadnezzar to swallow. He was the most powerful king of that day, and he had built a truly spectacular kingdom. He must have felt it would all last forever. He couldn't imagine that someday he would meet his end and his kingdom would fall.

As Daniel 2:21 proclaims, God "removes kings and raises up kings." The rulers of this world come and go. Each new ruler has their dreams and aspirations. He is convinced that his government will be different and greater than those that came before. He is confident that his power and authority will continue. But as time passes, every king and kingdom passes away from the scene.

In the end, it is the King of kings and Lord of lords who will reign forever—and His kingdom will endure for all eternity.

FAITH UNDER FIRE

DANIEL 3

No one defied Nebuchadnezzar. He was used to having his way. When he gave a command, people were quick to oblige. To say no to the king just wasn't done.

So when Daniel's three friends refused to bow to the golden statue, Nebuchadnezzar had to have been stunned. The price of disobedience was death by fire. Everyone in the massive crowd was quick to obey except for these three. It didn't make sense.

Though Nebuchadnezzar was outraged, he said he would give them a second chance. And if they didn't comply, he would throw them into a fiery furnace. Then with a mixture of arrogance and mockery, the king declared, "Who is the god who will deliver you from my hands?" (Daniel 3:15).

Nebuchadnezzar saw himself as so powerful that no god could overrule his actions—not even the one true God. He was convinced that nothing could deliver Shadrach, Meshach, and Abednego from a blazing furnace.

If the king thought that would get the three men to bow, he was wrong.

They said, "Our God whom we serve is able to deliver us from the burning fiery furnace, and He will deliver us from your hand, O king. But if not, let it be known to you, O king, that we do not serve your gods, nor will we worship the gold image which you have set up" (Daniel 3:17-18).

The three men had unshakeable confidence in God. They believed the Lord could deliver them. But even if He didn't, they would remain faithful to Him. Faced with the choice of pleasing God or pleasing man, it was no contest. They would choose God every time.

This is the confidence we should have as well. Whether God delivers us or not, we win when we are faithful to Him. No matter what our dilemma, we are safe in His hands. There is no safer place to be.

CAPTURE THE SCENE (What do I see?)

Using your Bible, answer the following questions.

1. Whom did Nebuchadnezzar command to take part in the worship of the gold statue (Daniel 3:2)?

2. What was the crowd ordered to do when the music started (verses 4-5)?

3. What fate would meet anyone who dared to disobey (verse 6)?

4. Who refused to bow (verse 12)?

5. What was Nebuchadnezzar's response (verses 15-16)?

6. What did Shadrach, Meshach, and Abednego say to King Nebuchadnez-zar (verses 16-19)?

7. In anger, what did Nebuchadnezzar command be done to the furnace (verse 19)?

8. What happened to the men who threw Shadrach, Meshach, and Abed-nego into the fire (verse 22)?

9. When the king looked into the furnace, how many men did he see walking in it, and how did he describe one of the men (verse 25)?

10. What did Nebuchadnezzar say about the God of Shadrach, Meshach, and Abednego when he saw that the fire had no power over the three men (verses 28-29)?

ANALYZE THE MESSAGE (What does it say and mean?)

Using both your Bible and your copy of the book *Discovering Daniel*, answer the following questions.

1. What do you think the creation of the tall statue revealed about Nebuchadnezzar (see page 62 in *Discovering Daniel*)?

2. According to Revelation 13:15-17, what future figure will also have an image created for the purpose of worship? What will happen to those who refuse to worship the image?

3. What sin caused the fall of Satan himself (see page 63 in *Discovering Daniel*)? How does Isaiah 14:12-14 describe the way this sin was expressed?

4. Daniel lists the types of people Nebuchadnezzar invited to the statue ceremony (see Daniel 3:2-3). What do you think the king hoped to accomplish by inviting these specific people?

5. Shadrach, Meshach, and Abednego were clear in their refusal to bow before the statue. They respectfully disregarded Nebuchadnezzar's authority. They defied his power and any sense of victory he might have over them. Why do you think they were so determined in their conviction?

6. When the three Jewish men said "But if not," were they expressing a lack of faith? Explain (see page 69 in *Discovering Daniel*).

7. When Nebuchadnezzar saw a fourth man in the furnace with the other three, he was likely witnessing a theophany. What is a theophany, and where else in Scripture do we see this (see page 71 in *Discovering Daniel*)?

8. God didn't prevent Shadrach, Meshach, and Abednego from being thrown into the fire. There are times when God allows us to experience trials by fire as well. Why would He do this (see page 72 in *Discovering Daniel*)?

9. What do you think God wanted to teach Nebuchadnezzar through this fiery furnace incident?

COMPARE THIS PASSAGE WITH THE REST OF SCRIPTURE
(How is it supported elsewhere in the Bible?)

1. Read Isaiah 43:2, then answer the questions below:

> When you pass through the waters, I will be with you;
> and through the rivers, they shall not overflow you.
> When you walk through the fire, you shall not be burned,
> nor shall the flame scorch you.

   a. Where did God say He would be during our trials?

b. In the above passage—or anywhere else in the Bible—does God ever say He will prevent us from experiencing difficult circumstances?

c. What are some ways we can benefit from life's trials?

2. Read Proverbs 4:23. An important aspect of living an uncompromising life is to "keep [your] heart with all diligence." List three or four ways we can guard our hearts.

3. Scripture gives many examples of people who gave in to the temptation to compromise. What consequences did the following individuals face by making the wrong choice?

a. Adam (Genesis 3:6, 22-24)—

b. Esau (Genesis 25:29-34)—

c. Saul (1 Samuel 15:3, 20-28)—

d. Solomon (1 Kings 11:1-8)—

e. Ananias and Sapphira (Acts 5:1-11)—

4. Based on the examples above, what conclusions do you come to about the dangers of compromise?

EXECUTE (How does this affect my life?)

1. On page 60 of *Discovering Daniel*, we read, "There are occupational hazards when it comes to following Christ. Chief among them is being despised by the world."

   a. What are some of the ways we can be despised for our faith?

   b. What are some other occupational hazards Christians face?

2. Read Acts 20:23-24. Why was the apostle Paul willing to suffer "bonds and afflictions"?

3. Jesus was with Shadrach, Meshach, and Abednego in the fiery furnace. What promises can we cling to when we find ourselves in the fiery furnaces of life?

   a. Matthew 28:20—

b. Hebrews 13:5—

4. Read 1 Peter 4:12-14.

a. How does Peter urge us to respond to fiery ordeals?

b. What benefits do we receive when we are ridiculed for Christ, according to verse 14?

CLOSING THOUGHTS

Down through the ages, martyrs have stood up to their persecutors to the point of death. And Shadrach, Meshach, and Abednego were prepared to lay down their lives for what they believed.

It was James who made this observation about genuine faith:

Someone will say, "You have faith, and I have works." Show me your faith without your works, and I will show you my faith by my works. You believe that there is one God. You do well. Even the demons believe—and tremble! But do you want to know, O foolish man, that faith without works is dead? (James 2:18-20).

Genuine faith is demonstrative faith. You can see it in action. It does not hide under the pretense that "my religious beliefs are private." True faith will express itself—whether by helping someone in time of need, praying for someone, counseling or encouraging a friend, or sharing Christ with your fellow workers. You cannot hide genuine faith. It always bursts forth in some type of action.

In relation to Scripture's call for us to be the salt and light of the world (Matthew 5:13-14), you may have heard this question asked: If you were accused of being a Christian, would there be enough evidence to convict you? Would others be able to point to specific ways you've made it evident you are a Christ follower? Or would they be hard-pressed to do that?

Fortunately, not many of us are faced with the possibility of death because of our faith (although there are many believers in other places around the world for whom death is a very real possibility because they are Christians). Yet sadly, we will find ourselves in situations where we're tempted to compromise our faith for the sake of not getting in trouble with the world. Even something as subtle as the temptation to stay quiet when we should speak the truth can trip us up.

Shadrach, Meshach, and Abednego could have taken the easy way out. They could have bowed down, like everyone else. But then Nebuchadnezzar would *never* have said, "There is no other God who can deliver like this" (Daniel 3:29).

You would think that by now—with the lessons of Daniel chapters 2 and 3 behind him—Nebuchadnezzar would know who really is in control of all things. But like many of us, he had to learn this lesson repeatedly. That's what we'll see in the next lesson.

LEARNING THE HARD WAY

DANIEL 4

Imagine how differently life would have been for King Nebuchadnezzar if he hadn't conquered Jerusalem and taken a large group of Jewish exiles back to Babylon, including Daniel, Shadrach, Meshach, and Abednego. It was because these young men were now among the king's advisors that a whole new world opened up for him.

Beforehand, all the king had known were the gods of Babylon. If he had ever been exposed to the one true God, we're not aware of it.

And from the time Nebuchadnezzar was crowned king, he had become used to the adulation and authority that comes with being ruler over all. The fact Babylon was the most powerful empire in the world also contributed to Nebuchadnezzar's perception of his own greatness. There was nothing to keep his pride in check.

But ever since Daniel and his friends had become part of the king's wise men, Nebuchadnezzar found himself coming face to face with the One who was more powerful than him, and more powerful than the gods of Babylon. He discovered that his wise men weren't all that wise, and that his kingdom would someday be taken over by another. He came to learn that the God Daniel worshipped is a God in heaven who can interpret dreams. And that same God was able to protect Shadrach, Meshach, and Abednego from the flames of a fiery furnace.

If Daniel and his friends hadn't been exiled to Babylon, King Nebuchadnezzar and others in his kingdom would have had far less exposure to the God of the universe.

Anytime we find ourselves in "exile"—that is, in difficult situations—we should remember that God can use us within those situations for His purposes. He desires to use us to influence others in ways we might never have anticipated. Just as God worked through Daniel to influence Nebuchadnezzar and his wise men, God can use us within life's hard circumstances to bring His light where He wants it to shine.

CAPTURE THE SCENE (What do I see?)

Using your Bible, answer the following questions.

1. What does Nebuchadnezzar proclaim in Daniel 4:1-3?

2. What reaction did Nebuchadnezzar have to a new dream that had come to him (verse 5)?

3. What happened when Nebuchadnezzar asked his wise men to interpret the dream (verse 7)?

4. Nebuchadnezzar then shared the details of the dream with Daniel. What did the king say about the tree that he saw in the dream (verses 10-12)?

5. What did a "watcher…from heaven" command be done to the tree (verses 14-15)?

6. What "sentence" did this watcher warn would be imposed upon Nebuchadnezzar (verse 16)?

7. How did Daniel react upon hearing the details of the dream? And who did Daniel wish the dream could have been about (verse 19)?

8. What did Daniel say the tree represented (verses 20-22)?

9. What did Daniel say the dream was foretelling about Nebuchadnezzar (verses 23-26)?

10. What warning did Daniel then give to the king (verse 27)?

11. A year later, what happened to King Nebuchadnezzar after he acted pridefully (verses 31-33)?

12. After a seven-year punishment, what did Nebuchadnezzar acknowledge about God (verses 34-37)?

ANALYZE THE MESSAGE (What does it say and mean?)

Using both your Bible and your copy of the book *Discovering Daniel*, answer the following questions.

1. Based on what you have read up to this point in *Discovering Daniel*:

    a. In what ways have you seen King Nebuchadnezzar exhibit his pride?

    b. In what ways have you seen Daniel exhibit humility?

    c. As you look at Nebuchadnezzar and Daniel side by side, what two or three dominant lessons do you think God wants to teach us through their examples?

2. At the beginning of Daniel 4, Nebuchadnezzar evidently has a brief moment of clarity about "the Most High God." What does he say about God in verses 2-3? And why is this such a stunning admission coming from Nebuchadnezzar?

3. What is significant about the fact the tree would be chopped down, but the stump would remain and not be cut to pieces (see page 85 in *Discovering Daniel*)? What does this tell us about God?

4. Through Nebuchadnezzar's punishment, we learn that God's patience is great, but is not unending. On page 92 of *Discovering Daniel*, we read that when hard times come to us, we should prayerfully evaluate whether we need to make changes in our life. As Amir says, "Whether the origin of our struggle is the disciplinary hand of God or just the fact that we are living in corruptible bodies in a fallen world, we can always learn from and grow through the pain."

   What are some things we can learn when God shows tough-love discipline toward us?

5. In Daniel 4:34-35, what truths does Nebuchadnezzar affirm about God? What thoughts go through your mind as you consider that these words came from the mouth of the most powerful man on Earth?

COMPARE THIS PASSAGE WITH THE REST OF SCRIPTURE
(How is it supported elsewhere in the Bible?)

1. After Nebuchadnezzar had his dream about the tree, he asked his wise men to help interpret the dream. This raises an interesting question: Why did the king turn to them when they had failed to interpret the dream recorded in Daniel 2? Why didn't Nebuchadnezzar go immediately to Daniel, who had a proven track record?

   We see this happen elsewhere in Scripture. In Genesis 12:13, when Abraham wanted to protect himself, he told Sarah to lie and say that she was his sister. Later, Abraham was rebuked for this. And yet what did Abraham do again in Genesis 20:2?

2. Why do you think we have a tendency to repeat our mistakes or sins instead of going to God first when we need help?

3. God detests pride. Ultimately, pride causes a person to put self before God. What do the following passages have to say about pride?

   a. Exodus 20:3—

b. Isaiah 48:11—

c. Proverbs 16:5—

4. Read Philippians 3:4-6. Before Paul became a Christian, what reasons could he give for boasting about himself?

5. After Paul became a believer, what did he say about his accomplishments (Philippians 3:7-9)?

6. Galatians 6:7 says, "Do not be deceived, God is not mocked; for whatever a man sows, that he will also reap."

a. Based on what we have read about Nebuchadnezzar so far, in what ways had he mocked God?

b. In what ways did he reap what he sowed?

c. What should we personally take to heart from Galatians 6:7?

EXECUTE (How does this affect my life?)

1. Proverbs 16:5 says, "Everyone proud in heart is an abomination to the LORD." That tells us how strongly God feels about pride. According to the following passages, what are among the consequences of pride?

   a. Proverbs 11:2—

   b. Proverbs 16:18—

   c. Proverbs 29:23—

2. Pride isn't always overt. Sometimes it can be subtle. What are some ways that it's possible for us to be prideful without noticing it?

3. According to James 4:6, how does God react to the proud? To the humble?

4. What perspective does Psalm 121:1-2 encourage us to cultivate?

5. Many of us are familiar with Proverbs 3:5-6: "Trust in the LORD with all your heart, and lean not on your own understanding; in all your ways acknowledge Him, and He shall direct your paths." Typically we think of this passage in terms of *dependence* upon God, but it's also an exhortation for us to express *humility*. Biblically, there is a connection between dependence and humility.

   a. To what extent does verse 5 tell us to trust God?

b. To what extent does verse 6 urge us to acknowledge Him?

c. In light of what verses 5 and 6 say, do you think there are any exceptions? Why or why not?

6. The Lord Jesus Christ is entirely deserving of our reverence, worship, and obedience. He is worthy of the highest exaltation and praise. Yet in Philippians 2:5-8, we read this:

> Jesus, who being in the form of God, did not consider it robbery to be equal with God, but made Himself of no reputation, taking the form of a bondservant, and coming in the likeness of men. And being found in appearance as a man, He humbled Himself and became obedient to the point of death, even the death of the cross.

Christ's humility came at a high price. Yet He was willing because of the good that would come from descending Himself. The apostle Paul urges us to follow Christ's example by saying, "Let this mind be in you which was also in Christ Jesus" (verse 5).

a. What are some examples of the cost we may pay for being humble?

b. What are some benefits we and others can gain when we're willing to be humble?

CLOSING THOUGHTS

As we read about Nebuchadnezzar, it would be easy for us to say, "Why did he keep making the same mistake again and again? I wouldn't do that."

But with a bit of thought, we should be able to think of ways we've grieved God repeatedly. We haven't always learned a lesson as quickly as we should. Even as believers, we find ourselves succumbing to certain sins time and again. Even after nearly 30 years as a Christian, the great apostle Paul wrote, "I do not understand my own actions. For I do not do what I want, but I do the very thing I hate" (Romans 7:15). That describes all of us, doesn't it? Temptation beckons at us, we choose to do wrong rather than right, and we get frustrated. And we wonder why we can't overcome certain behaviors once and for all.

It is for this reason that we can be grateful we have a patient God. Psalm 103:8 says, "The LORD is merciful and gracious, slow to anger and abounding in steadfast love."

Yet at the same time, we don't want to fall into the mindset that we can stretch God's patience just a bit more. In Romans 2:4, Paul wrote, "Do you presume on the riches of [God's] kindness and forbearance and patience, not knowing that God's kindness is meant to lead you to repentance?"

The intent of God's patience is that we would take corrective action. Also, as Hebrews 12:6 says, "The Lord disciplines the one he loves." This is made evident in the lives of many people in Scripture. May God's loving rebukes of their wrong attitudes and actions serve as loving exhortations for us to exhibit right attitudes and actions!

THE END OF AN EMPIRE

DANIEL 5

The sounds of laughter and singing turned into gasps and murmurs. The party guests had never seen anything like this. Moments earlier, they had been uninhibited and festive. Now they were filled with crippling fear.

The queen, who evidently was not at the banquet, could hear the loud voices of panic from elsewhere in the palace. She had to see this for herself. She quickly made her way to the massive banquet hall. Upon entering, she saw the king, who was pale and trembling. She saw that everyone was staring at and pointing to a wall upon which had been written four cryptic words. She quickly assessed the reason the partygoers were so alarmed.

The queen greeted the king with the proper salutation, then declared, "Do not let your thoughts trouble you, nor let your countenance change" (Daniel 5:10). She knew the answer to King Belshazzar's dilemma: Daniel.

The queen continued: "There is a man in your kingdom in whom is the Spirit of the Holy God" (verse 11). She then explained that this man—whom Nebuchadnezzar had made chief of the wise men—could interpret dreams, solve riddles, and explain enigmas. She urged that Belshazzar bring him into the room to interpret the handwriting on the wall.

The more the queen said about Daniel, the more the king remembered that yes, there was a wise man in the kingdom who was above all the others.

Under normal circumstances, this king wouldn't have cared to hear from Daniel. But this wasn't a normal circumstance. The handwriting on the wall had frightened everyone at the banquet. As their king, he had to figure out how to calm them. So he was willing to do whatever was necessary to solve this disturbing mystery. Perhaps this Daniel could calm everyone's fears.

Like Belshazzar, there are many people today who ignore God and want nothing to do with Him until tragedy hits them. At first, they will look to their gods of silver and gold, prestige and position, or self-determination and personal resolve. But ultimately, all those gods will fail them. And the longer the crisis lingers, the more desperate they will get. Only when they have no other choice do they decide to turn to God or to someone who knows God.

As long as such people have control over all that is happening in their lives, they see no need for God. It is only when a situation is beyond their ability to solve it that they reluctantly bring God into the picture. That was where Belshazzar found himself.

Imagine what Daniel must have thought and felt when he walked into that hall. A quick look around showed a depth of debauchery that was grievous and appalling. And a glance at the handwriting on the wall told him that judgment was imminent. The king was about to lose his kingdom, and rightly so. Belshazzar's knees were still shaking as he asked Daniel to read the writing. He promised Daniel a great reward, which was ludicrous considering the meaning of the four words MENE, MENE, TEKEL, UPHARSIN. Little did the king realize those words spelled his doom—that very night.

CAPTURE THE SCENE (What do I see?)

Using your Bible, answer the following questions.

1. Who was at Belshazzar's feast, and what were the people doing that showed contempt for God (see Daniel 5:1-4)?

2. What suddenly appeared, and how did the king react (verses 5-6)?

3. Whom did the king call upon to interpret the writing, and what was the result (verses 7-9)?

4. What did the queen suggest that the king do, and why (verses 10-12)?

5. How did the king greet Daniel, and what did he promise if Daniel could read the writing (verses 13-16)?

6. What was Daniel's response to the king's promise of reward (verse 17)?

7. Briefly, what did Daniel then say about King Nebuchadnezzar (verses 18-21)?

8. What did Daniel condemn Belshazzar for (verses 22-23)?

9. What did the words on the wall say (verses 24-28)?

10. What happened later that night (verses 30-31)?

ANALYZE THE MESSAGE (What does it say and mean?)

Using both your Bible and your copy of the book *Discovering Daniel*, answer the following questions.

1. Where had the gold and silver vessels that King Belshazzar used in his feast come from (see Daniel 5:2-3)?

2. How did God react to His sacred vessels being used in such a flippant manner (see page 104 in *Discovering Daniel*)?

3. As we read the account of what happened in the banquet hall, what clues are we given about the fear and desperation felt by Belshazzar and the partygoers (see verses 6-9)?

4. What does the fact Belshazzar had to be reminded about Daniel's past exploits tell you about Belshazzar?

5. What does Daniel's rejection of the king's offer of rewards tell you about Daniel's motives and priorities?

6. What does the meaning of the four words MENE, MENE, TEKEL, UPHARSIN—as well as the swiftness of the judgment that followed— tell us about how God felt toward Belshazzar?

7. Why do you think Daniel was willing to speak so boldly against King Belshazzar, even though that could mean a death sentence?

8. For what three reasons did the king sit there and take Daniel's words (see page 110 in *Discovering Daniel*)?

COMPARE THIS PASSAGE WITH THE REST OF SCRIPTURE
(How is it supported elsewhere in the Bible?)

It's hard to imagine how a kingdom as mighty as Babylon would fall so quickly and thoroughly. But it was because the king and the empire's leaders did not realize the seriousness of their situation. Physically, morally, and spiritually, they had failed to recognize how vulnerable they had become. So confident were they in Babylon's mighty walls that they had not noticed the natural threat that the Medo-Persian Empire posed. So preoccupied were they with self-pleasure and sin that they had disregarded the threat that a supernatural and angry God posed.

The wickedness of Babylon had escalated to the point that God's patience ran out. It was time for judgment. We see this scenario played out elsewhere in the Bible. Let's look at four key examples:

1. The Flood (Genesis 6–7)

    a. What does Genesis 6:5 tell us mankind was like during the days of Noah?

b. What did God resolve to do (see verse 7)?

c. Did anyone outside of Noah's family come to repentance and join them on the ark (see Genesis 7:7)?

2. Sodom and Gomorrah (Genesis 18–19)

a. What did God say about Sodom and Gomorrah in Genesis 18:20?

b. In Genesis 19:12-13, what warning was given to Lot and his family about Sodom and Gomorrah, and why?

c. What judgment did God pour out upon the two cities and the surrounding area (see verse 24)?

3. Babylon the Great—Revelation 18

   a. How does an angel describe the sins of Babylon the Great, the political and economic system of the Antichrist (see verses 2-3)?

   b. What did another voice say about the sins of Babylon (see verse 5)?

   c. How quickly are we told that Babylon's judgment will take place (see verse 8)?

4. The World in Our Day—2 Timothy 3:1-5

   In 2 Timothy 3:1-5, the apostle Paul warned what mankind would be like as we approach the end times:

   > Know this, that in the last days perilous times will come: For men will be lovers of themselves, lovers of money, boasters, proud, blasphemers, disobedient to parents, unthankful, unholy, unloving, unforgiving, slanderers, without self-control, brutal, despisers of good, traitors, headstrong, haughty, lovers of pleasure rather than lovers of God, having a form of godliness but denying its power.

The description given here fits all too well with the world around us today, doesn't it? As has happened in the past, God's patience will eventually run out. Second Chronicles 36:16 reports how, before the Babylonian captivity, the southern kingdom of Judah had reached the point of no return: "They mocked the messengers of God, despised His words, and scoffed at His prophets, until the wrath of the LORD arose against His people, till there was no remedy."

"Till there is no remedy" is the clincher. The world we live in is rapidly approaching this point. And once again, God will say what He spoke in Genesis 6:3 before sending the flood: "My Spirit shall not strive with man forever."

EXECUTE (How does this affect my life?)

1. What are some ways that we as Christians test the patience of God?

2. What question does the apostle Paul ask in Romans 6:1? And how does he answer in verse 2?

3. What exhortations are we given in the following passages?

   a. 2 Corinthians 13:5—

b. 2 Peter 1:10-11—

c. 1 Thessalonians 5:21-22—

4. Why do you think frequent self-introspection is so important for us as believers?

5. What is God's will for us, according to 1 Thessalonians 4:3-5?

6. What call are we given in Romans 12:1-2?

7. Why do you think God so greatly desires for us to pursue purity and Christlikeness?

CLOSING THOUGHTS

King Belshazzar had an "appointed time" that God would give, then take away. According to Psalm 139:16, every person's days were written in God's book before they were born. This is true of all of us. God is the One who numbers our days on the earth. He determines how much time He will give us to carry out His will. But too often, we don't use the opportunities He places before us, and the windows close on those opportunities.

Think about the times in your life when God gave you a window of opportunity to do something for Him but you didn't follow through. Perhaps you were afraid of failure, or you were concerned about what other people would think. Or, like Moses, you focused too much on the question, "Who am I?" (Exodus 3:11). And then that window of opportunity closed, and you missed out on blessing others—and you missed the blessing God had intended to give you for obedience.

But the judgment faced by believers will be very different from the judgment faced by unbelievers. That's because Christ has already paid the price for our sins. He has already faced God's wrath on our behalf. Salvation is a free gift, "not a result of works" (Ephesians 2:9). Through Christ, we have been made right before God. As Romans 8:1 says, "There is therefore now no condemnation for those who are in Christ Jesus."

While our *salvation* is secure and absolutely assured, there is a judgment we will face that determines the rewards we will receive in heaven. Romans 14:10 speaks of the day when "we shall all stand before the judgment seat of Christ." First Corinthians 3:11-14 tells us the purpose of this event, at which "fire will test what sort of work each one has done":

> No other foundation can anyone lay than that which is laid, which is Jesus Christ. Now if anyone builds on this foundation with gold, silver, precious stones, wood hay, straw, each one's work will become clear; for the Day will declare it, because it will be revealed by fire; and the fire will test each one's work, of what sort it is. If anyone's work which he has built on it endures, he will receive a reward.

This fire will reveal whether our service to the Lord was comprised of gold, silver, and precious stones, or wood, hay, and straw. Will our service to God consist of things that last for eternity, or things that are temporary and destined for destruction?

When King Belshazzar was weighed in God's balance of humility, justice, mercy, and righteousness, Belshazzar ranked a zero. He was not humble, nor did he show anyone true justice or mercy, nor did he reign in righteousness.

One day, all believers will stand before Christ and be weighed in the balance. The purpose will be for our Lord to reward us for the ways we used the gifts and opportunities He gave to us so that we would bless others.

The apostle Paul lovingly exhorts us to be mindful of how we use our time here on Earth. In Ephesians 5:16, he says, "See that you walk circumspectly, not as fools but as wise, redeeming the time because the days are evil." And in Philippians 2:12-13, he writes, "As you have always obeyed, not as in my presence only, but now much more in my absence, work out your own salvation with fear and trembling; for it is God who works in you both to will and to do for His good pleasure."

When Paul says we are to "work out" our salvation, he is not saying salvation is by works. Rather, he is saying we are to live out what is true about us internally: that we are children of God. As those who have been declared righteous by God, we should live accordingly.

OPEN MOUTHS, CLOSED MOUTHS

DANIEL 6

O f all the wise men in Babylon, Daniel had made the greatest contributions to the good of the empire. For several decades, he served King Nebuchadnezzar faithfully. He exercised his authority with integrity. In the times when God desired to rebuke and warn the king, Daniel didn't flinch. He said what God wanted the king to hear. For this reason, the king knew he could trust Daniel. He was a favorite of the king.

So stellar was Daniel's reputation that he continued in his role after King Darius conquered Babylon for the Medes and Persians. In fact, Daniel distinguished himself so greatly that Darius thought about "setting him over the whole realm" (Daniel 6:3). Once again, Daniel was a favorite. Evidently this made Daniel's fellow governors and satraps (or administrators) envious.

By this time, Daniel was in his eighties. So impeccable was his character that when the jealous governors and satraps plotted his downfall, they couldn't find any error or fault in him. They couldn't accuse him of any wrongdoing.

They realized there was only one way they could get rid of Daniel: By making it a crime for him to remain faithful to God.

In this story, we see how people with wicked motives lose their ability to think and act logically. The jealousy of Daniel's fellow administrators so blinded them that they were willing to resort to evil to destroy good. In a twist of irony, those who were eager to condemn Daniel did deeds worthy of condemnation. And the cruelty they exhibited is stunning. They had no hesitations about throwing an elderly and physically fragile man into a pit of hungry lions.

Daniel's enemies had come up with such an airtight plot that Daniel's end was sure.

Or so they thought.

CAPTURE THE SCENE (What do I see?)

Using your Bible, answer the following questions.

1. As Darius set up governors and administrators over the kingdom, what did he think about doing, and why (see Daniel 6:3)?

2. How did the other governors and satraps feel about Daniel (see verses 4-5)?

3. Those who were plotting against Daniel were able to convince King Darius to sign a decree. What law did this decree establish (see verses 7-9)?

4. What did Daniel do upon learning the decree had been signed (see verse 10)?

5. What did Daniel's accusers catch him doing (see verse 11)? And what did they say to the king (see verses 11-14)?

6. What was the king's reaction when he realized a trap had been set for Daniel (see verse 14)?

7. Because the law could not be retracted, what was the king forced to do (see verses 15-17)?

8. What happened to the king during the night, and what did he do first thing in the morning (see verses 18-20)?

9. What was Daniel's response to the king (see verses 21-22)?

10. What did the king command be done to Daniel's accusers, and what was their fate (see verse 24)?

11. King Darius then wrote a new decree. What did the decree say about God (see verses 26-27)?

ANALYZE THE MESSAGE (What does it say and mean?)

Using both your Bible and your copy of the book *Discovering Daniel,* answer the following questions.

1. Daniel's fellow governors and administrators did not like the idea of being placed under his authority. Knowing what you do about Daniel's character, what are some reasons these adversaries were so determined to get rid of Daniel (see page 115 in *Discovering Daniel*)?

2. Why do you think King Darius was able to be persuaded to sign the new law?

3. In light of the new law, Daniel could have changed his prayer routine, but didn't. What are some reasons you can think of for why Daniel continued his habit of prayer?

4. When King Darius was forced to have Daniel thrown into the lions' den, he made this remarkable statement to Daniel: "Your God, whom you serve continually, He will deliver you" (Daniel 6:16). By this time, Daniel would have served Darius for at least a year or two. What might Daniel have done during that time that would impress upon the king the idea that God might deliver Daniel?

5. In Daniel 6:22, whom did Daniel credit for protecting him from the lions?

6. Why do you think the account about Daniel in the lions' den generates such a strongly positive and empathetic response from those who read it?

COMPARE THIS PASSAGE WITH THE REST OF SCRIPTURE
(How is it supported elsewhere in the Bible?)

1. The fact King Darius sentenced Daniel's accusers to the very same sentence they had imposed upon Daniel may seem harsh. But note the Old Testament principle taught in the following passages:

   a. What does Deuteronomy 19:16-21 state was to be done with those who bore false witness?

   b. After Haman was caught conspiring to have the innocent Mordecai hanged on the gallows, what fate did Haman face, according to Esther 7:9-10?

   c. In Obadiah 15, what did God say He would do to the nations that harm His people?

2. Have you noticed by now that whenever Daniel was opposed or persecuted by enemies, he never avenged them? What attitudes are we to have toward our enemies, according to the following passages?

a. Matthew 5:44—

b. Romans 12:17-19—

c. Romans 12:20—

EXECUTE (How does this affect my life?)

1. When we as Christians are faithful to God, we can expect opposition. What do you think are among the reasons that unbelievers respond negatively toward us?

2. Read 1 Peter 3:13-17 and answer the following:

    a. What happens when we suffer "for righteousness' sake" (verse 14)?

    b. Rather than be afraid, what are we to do, according to verse 15?

    c. What can our good conscience and good conduct do to those who oppose us?

    d. What distinction is Peter careful to make in verse 17?

3. On page 121 of *Discovering Daniel*, we read this:

    In your time of trial, even though you don't see a physical manifestation of the Almighty God, do you still believe that He loves you, that He is watching out for you, and that He will always see and reward your righteousness?

Why can we be confident God is watching out for us even when it seems He hasn't come to our rescue? Are there Bible passages you can use to support your answer?

4. In what ways does Daniel's example inspire you to grow more?

CLOSING THOUGHTS

The fact God delivered Daniel from the lions confirms that He is able to care for His own in miraculous ways. But we shouldn't take that to mean He will always rescue us from trouble. In Scripture, there are many instances in which God did not bring deliverance to His own. For example, in Hebrews 11:35-38, we read of faithful saints who

> were tortured, not accepting deliverance, that they might obtain a better resurrection. Still others had trial of mockings and scourgings, yes, and of chains and imprisonment. They were stoned, they were sawn in two, were tempted, were slain with the sword. They wandered in sheepskins and goatskins, being destitute, afflicted, tormented...They wandered in deserts and mountains, in dens and caves of the earth.

Many times, we won't understand how or why, but God will have purposes for letting us experience rejection, opposition, or persecution. It's important to observe that James 1:12 says, "Blessed is the one who *perseveres* under trial" (NIV). Note that James said "perseveres," and not "escapes" or "avoids." We are blessed when we endure, not when we evade.

A bit earlier in that same chapter, James says you can be confident in your trials, "knowing that the testing of your faith produces patience. But let patience have its perfect work, that you may be perfect and complete, lacking nothing" (verses 3-4). When our faith is tested, we can know good results.

In 2 Corinthians 4:8-10, Paul confirms this key purpose for our suffering:

> We are hard-pressed on every side, yet not crushed; we are perplexed, but not in despair, persecuted, but not forsaken; struck down, but not destroyed—always carrying about in the body the dying of the Lord Jesus, *that the life of Christ also may be manifested in our body* (emphasis added).

Our suffering enables us to magnify Christ. When we endure opposition, we can make the Lord visible through us. The strength we exhibit as we persevere makes it possible for our enemies to see God at work in us. They won't have any other explanation for why we are able to exhibit strength and courage even as we are weak and in pain.

A little later, in verse 15, Paul affirms that "all things are for your sakes, that grace, having spread through the many, may cause thanksgiving to abound to the glory of God." Our hardships can put God on display, leading people to experience His grace and give glory to Him.

If God should choose *not* to deliver us when we face opposition, we can know with certainty that He will use our difficult circumstance to do a good work in our own lives and in the lives of others.

THE BEGINNING OF VISIONS

DANIEL 7

In Daniel 7, we read that the elderly prophet has a dream that has similarities to the one King Nebuchadnezzar had long ago in Daniel 2. In both dreams, there are four earthly and temporary kingdoms, followed by a fifth and eternal kingdom.

But there are also differences.

Nebuchadnezzar saw a statue that presented a succession of world empires in all their splendor. He looked ahead into history from a human perspective. As he did so, emphasis is placed on the temporary nature of the kingdoms of Earth and their human rulers. Then came "a stone…cut out without hands" that destroyed the entire statue so that "no trace" remained (Daniel 2:34-35). This depicts Christ's future kingdom replacing all the earthly ones. To Nebuchadnezzar, this seemed a disruptive ending.

In contrast, Daniel saw four wild beasts that represented the same four earthly kingdoms that Nebuchadnezzar saw, only this time from God's perspective. Daniel's descriptions of the beasts reveal the sinister character of these kingdoms. In fact, Daniel was troubled by what he saw—especially when it came to the fourth beast, "which was different from all the others, exceedingly dreadful," and would go on to make "war against the saints" (7:19, 21).

But then the four beasts were followed by a vision of God's throne room.

This is a scene of judgment. Here, the splendor is God in all His glory. The emphasis is clearly on the final kingdom, which is eternal. God's sovereign power is on grand display here—a power that is supreme and everlasting.

CAPTURE THE SCENE (What do I see?)

Using your Bible, answer the following questions.

1. When did Daniel's dream occur, and what did he first see (Daniel 7:1-2)?

2. Daniel saw four beasts. Give a brief description of each one:

   a. First beast (verse 4)—

   b. Second beast (verse 5)—

   c. Third beast (verse 6)—

d. Fourth beast (verse 7)—

3. How many horns did the fourth beast have, and what does the little horn that rises among them do (verses 8-9)?

4. Who does Daniel see in verse 9, and what do we see in the surrounding scene, according to verse 10?

5. What happens to the horn (or beast) in verse 11, and to the fellow beasts in verse 12?

6. Briefly, what do we read about the Son of Man in verses 13-14?

7. How did Daniel respond to the visions he saw (verse 15)?

8. What interpretation was Daniel given about the four beasts and the kingdom that follows them (verses 17-18)?

9. What will the fourth beast do, according to the last part of verse 20 and verses 23-25?

10. What will happen after the court is seated (verses 26-27)?

ANALYZE THE MESSAGE (What does it say and mean?)

Using both your Bible and your copy of the book *Discovering Daniel*, answer the following questions.

1. As you look at the description of the first three beasts in Daniel 7:4-6, what clues do you see that would help to explain why Daniel was troubled?

2. The fourth beast is described in verses 7-8. What clues do you see here that would explain why this beast was especially disturbing to Daniel?

3. In what ways do you see Daniel's awe and reverence made evident as he describes the Ancient of Days in verses 9-10?

4. Reading verses 9-10 again, what aspects of this description convey that the Ancient of Days is powerful and authoritative?

5. Both Daniel 7:11 and Revelation 19:20 describe the judgment and punishment of the Antichrist. How do you think the tone or nature of Daniel's vision would have changed at this key point, with the transition from evil worldly powers to a righteous heavenly power? Yet even with this revelation, why do you think Daniel felt so shaken after the dream was over?

6. In Daniel 7:13-14, we see the Son of Man enter the presence of the Ancient of Days. In what other Bible passage do we see these two meet (see pages 140-141 in *Discovering Daniel*)? What similarities do you see about the Son of Man in both passages?

7. For what two reasons is it foolish for unbelievers to assume they will have enough time to get right with God before they die (see page 149 in *Discovering Daniel*)?

8. As you read Daniel 7:26-27, in what ways do you see the Lord's sovereignty clearly stated?

COMPARE THIS PASSAGE WITH THE REST OF SCRIPTURE
(How is it supported elsewhere in the Bible?)

1. What do the following passages tell us about the nature and extent of God's sovereignty?

   a. Job 42:2—

b. Psalm 115:3—

c. Proverbs 21:1—

d. Isaiah 46:9-10—

2. In what ways are you encouraged by the above passages?

3. What do the following passages inform us about the Lord's future judgments against Satan, the Antichrist, and unbelievers?

a. 2 Thessalonians 1:8-9—

b. Hebrews 9:27—

c. Revelation 19:20—

d. Revelation 20:10—

e. Revelation 20:12-15—

4. What comforting truth do we find given to believers in Romans 8:1?

EXECUTE (How does this affect my life?)

1. Think back upon what you've read about Daniel in the previous chapters of *Discovering Daniel*. Consider his choices about not eating the king's food, about how to handle the interpretation of Nebuchadnezzar's dream, about being forthright to Belshazzar about the message written on the wall, and about the law regarding prayer to King Darius (and the penalty of being thrown into the lions' den). In what ways did Daniel show an immovable trust in God's sovereignty, and how God would sustain him in those difficult situations?

2. What are some ways you've shown a lack of confidence in God's sovereignty in past situations you've faced?

3. What are some ways that we, as believers, can demonstrate our trust in God's sovereignty when it seems things are out of control?

4. Daniel 7 includes a court scene and makes it clear that God will not let the Antichrist and the enemies of God's people go unpunished. In what ways does this truth comfort you?

5. In Romans 12:19, we are told, "Do not avenge yourselves, but rather give place to wrath; for it is written, 'Vengeance is Mine, I will repay,' says the Lord."

   a. Why do you think God wants us to let go of any thoughts of avenging others?

   b. Would you agree there is a freedom that comes from leaving vengeance in God's hands? Why or why not?

   c. What do the following passages tell you about the fairness of God's judgment?

      1) Romans 2:11—

      2) Colossians 3:25—

      3) 1 Peter 1:17—

Someday, we who are believers will come before the judgment seat of Christ (Romans 14:10). We are at no risk of losing our salvation because Christ has fully paid the penalty for our sins. Our salvation and eternal place in heaven are secure. But we'll be judged for our service to the Lord (1 Corinthians 3:12-15) and rewarded accordingly. If God is an all-knowing and impartial judge, we can have confidence that He will judge us lovingly and fairly.

CLOSING THOUGHTS

In Daniel 7, the part of the dream that bothered Daniel the most is the part that has not been fulfilled yet. It is still future. During the end times, the Antichrist will establish a global empire that is rampant with deception, blasphemy, and evil. As we read what Scripture says about the world's final ruler, we cannot help but feel great dread about the vicious manner in which he will exercise his power.

That's why it's so fitting that the Antichrist is called "the beast" in Revelation 13.

Throughout Scripture, we are given several glimpses of the extent of this world leader's depravity. In 2 Thessalonians chapter 2, he is described as "the man of sin...the son of perdition" (verse 3). He will exalt himself above God and go so far as to claim that he is God (verse 4). He is called "the lawless one...according to the working of Satan" (verse 9). In fact, Revelation 13:2 tells us that Satan will give the Antichrist "his power, his throne, and great authority." The Antichrist's power will come directly from Satan himself.

So cruel will the Antichrist be that he will "make war with the saints" (Revelation 13:7). He will have his right-hand man, the false prophet, kill anyone who refuses to worship him (verse 15). And he will forbid people from being able to buy and sell unless they swear allegiance to him (verses 16-17). This will lead to mass starvation and deprivation. In Daniel 8, we read that he will "destroy fearfully" and "cause deceit to prosper under his rule" (verses 24-25).

No wonder Daniel was so bothered.

You may have heard about world organizations that are advocating a "great reset" in an effort to solve global problems. Well, the Antichrist will bring about a great reset that is much more devastating than we can imagine. He will plunge mankind into the most frightening depths of moral and spiritual darkness—to the point that all hell breaks out on planet Earth as never before.

Thankfully, God has already set a limit on the length of the Antichrist's rule. The tribulation will last for seven years, and no longer. When that time is up, Christ will return. He will descend from heaven to Earth, and out of His mouth will come "a sharp sword, that with it He should strike the nations" (Revelation 19:15). In an instant, He will utterly destroy the Antichrist and all his forces.

And as Daniel 7:14 promises, Christ's kingdom will be "an everlasting dominion, which shall not pass away."

THE RAM AND THE GOAT

DANIEL 8

As we approach Daniel 8, we must again remind ourselves that as we read the prophecies given in the chapter, we have the advantage of hindsight. Looking back, we know that the vision in which Daniel saw the ram and the goat refers to the powerful Medo-Persian Empire and its conquest by the rapidly moving forces of the Greek Empire. For us, this is past history, and it can be difficult for us to appreciate the impact the vision had on Daniel because so many major shifts in world power have taken place since.

But in the vision, Daniel was looking ahead to history that had not happened yet. What he saw was frightening because of the mighty and devastating scale on which these events would take place. All of this was unprecedented. Never before had the world seen such massive armies and ruthless devastation.

The Medo-Persian Empire succeeded in defeating its enemies by overwhelming force. Its armies were so large they secured victory by sheer force of numbers. Up to that time in history, the Achaemenid Persian Empire became the largest the world had ever seen. It was seemingly invincible—until Alexander the Great came along.

Alexander was legendary for his military prowess. He had the ability to assess and exploit his enemies' weaknesses. Also significant was the speed at which he moved his extraordinarily efficient army of nearly 35,000 men. Estimates vary, but in the span of about a dozen years, he and his army marched many thousands of miles and captured, won over, or founded approximately 70 cities. Beforehand, no one would have ever believed that the entire Persian Empire—and lands beyond—would be defeated and collapse in such a short period of time. At its height, the Greek Empire stretched across roughly two million square miles over three continents.

So it's appropriate that in Daniel's vision, the male goat—the Greek Empire—is seen galloping "across the surface of the whole earth, without touching the ground" (8:5). And the vision correctly foresaw that the ram—the Medo-Persian Empire—would have "no power" to "withstand" the goat (verse 7).

From there, "the male goat grew very great" (verse 8). "But when he became strong, the large horn was broken, and in place of it four notable ones came up toward the four winds of heaven" (verse 9). At the peak of his strength and conquests, Alexander the Great died suddenly—the "large horn was broken." From there, all descended into chaos and anarchy, and his empire was split by four of his generals.

Again, looking back, all this makes sense to us. The details of Daniel's vision fit perfectly with what happened historically. But for Daniel, these events were still well into the future, and they were extremely unlike anything that had happened up till that time.

Not only that, but Daniel was given glimpses of the far future and the much-more distant future as well. He saw the rise of Antiochus IV, and more than 2,000 years later, the arrival of the end times and the world's final emperor, the Antichrist—the most satanic, ruthless, and murderous world leader ever. It's no wonder that after all he had seen, this dear prophet "was astonished" (verse 27). He was astounded by the enormity of what would take place, and the extent of the evil that would be unleashed.

CAPTURE THE SCENE (What do I see?)

Using your Bible, answer the following questions. As you do this, keep in mind that some of what is stated in Daniel's vision is difficult to understand, so it's okay to simply write your observations without fully grasping the meaning behind the descriptions.

1. What details does Daniel give to us about the ram (the Medo-Persian Empire) in Daniel 8:3-4?

2. What important fact does Daniel state about the goat (the Greek Empire) in verse 5?

3. What does the goat do to the ram in verses 6-7?

4. What then happens to the goat in verses 8-9?

5. By the time we reach verse 10, Daniel is taken further into the future. What do we see happen in the following verses, and what impressions do you get with regard to power and evil?

   a. Verse 10—

b. Verse 11—

c. Verse 12—

6. Who do we meet in verse 16, and what does he say to Daniel in verse 19?

7. What basic outline of history does Gabriel provide in verses 20-22?

8. In verses 23-25, we're introduced to "a king...having fierce features." Briefly, what are we told about this king?

9. What was Daniel told to do with the vision, and why (verse 26)?

10. What was Daniel's physical and mental response to the vision (verse 27)?

ANALYZE THE MESSAGE (What does it say and mean?)

Using both your Bible and your copy of the book *Discovering Daniel*, answer the following questions.

1. In Daniel 8:4, we read this about the Medo-Persian Empire: "I saw the ram pushing westward, northward, and southward, so that no animal could withstand him; nor was there any that could deliver from his hand, but he did according to his will." What does this reveal to us about the nature and power of the Medo-Persian Empire?

2. In Daniel 8:5, we're told this about the Greek Empire: The goat "attacked the ram…There was no power in the ram to withstand him…and there was no one that could deliver the ram." What do we learn here about the Medo-Persian Empire and the subsequent Greek Empire?

3. According to Daniel 8, what then suddenly happened to the Greek Empire?

4. What do we learn here about the seemingly most invincible world powers? Why is this important for us to keep in mind today?

5. In Daniel 8:23-25, we read about the wicked ruler Antiochus IV, who foreshadows the final world dictator, the Antichrist. Read these verses again with this in mind: Here, we see Antiochus's transgressions against and contempt for (1) the Jewish people and (2) God. What specific acts did this evil madman carry out against the Jews and God?

6. In Daniel 8:25, we're told Antiochus—and this will be true of the Antichrist as well—would "be broken *without human means*" (emphasis added). Ultimately, who will destroy Antiochus and the Antichrist?

COMPARE THIS PASSAGE WITH THE REST OF SCRIPTURE
(How is it supported elsewhere in the Bible?)

1. What specific points do the following passages make about God's sovereignty over people, including human kings and the extent of their rule?

   a. Job 14:5—

b. Psalm 75:6-7—

c. Daniel 2:21—

d. Daniel 4:35—

e. Acts 17:26—

2. With regard to God's sovereignty over our lives and the time He grants to us, what encouragement can we receive from these passages?

a. Psalm 73:23-24—

b. Isaiah 41:13—

c. Isaiah 46:4—

d. Hebrews 13:5—

EXECUTE (How does this affect my life?)

1. One of the challenges of living in a fallen world is that so often, we see the wicked prosper, while the righteous face struggles. Life seems so unjust.

   a. Read Psalm 73:3-9. In what ways do evil people seem to do well, and how are their attitudes described?

   b. But what is the eventual destiny of the wicked, according to verses 18-19?

c. In verses 27 and 28, what contrast do we see between those who reject God and those who embrace Him?

d. In light of the above, what long-term attitudes should we have about the prosperity of the wicked and the struggles faced by the righteous?

2. Bible prophecy tells us that both Antiochus IV and the Antichrist will persecute God's people. And even today, as we draw closer to the end times, it is becoming more difficult than ever to live as Christians in a world that has no moral or spiritual compass. With that in mind, what helpful wisdom do we gain from the following passages?

a. Matthew 5:10-12—

b. Matthew 5:44—

c. 2 Corinthians 12:9-10—

d. 2 Timothy 1:12—

e. 1 Peter 3:17—

3. In 2 Corinthians 4:17-18, the apostle Paul wrote these wonderful words:

> Our light affliction, which is but for a moment, is working for us
> a far more exceeding and eternal weight of glory, while we do not
> look at the things which are seen, but at the things which are not
> seen. For the things which are seen are temporary, but the things
> which are not seen are eternal.

How are you encouraged by this passage? And what are some ways we can remind ourselves to take our eyes off our momentary afflictions and keep them focused on the things that are eternal?

CLOSING THOUGHTS

The days of the Medo-Persian Empire, the Greek Empire, and Antiochus IV are long gone. Every prophecy given by Daniel about past kingdoms and leaders has been fulfilled with remarkable precision.

Yet there is still another tyrant who will emerge in the days to come. In Daniel 9:27, we read that he will make a seven-year peace treaty with Israel. But halfway through that period, he will break the treaty, enter the temple, set himself up as God, and demand the worship of people all over the globe. Daniel 11:36-37 tells us this figure "shall exalt and magnify himself above every god, shall speak blasphemies against the God of gods…He shall regard neither the God of his fathers…for he shall exalt himself above them all."

The advance glimpses we get of this world ruler in the book of Daniel line up with what we read about the Antichrist in Revelation 13. Yes, they are the same person. And if it appears as though he possesses supernatural power, it is because he will be energized by Satan (Revelation 13:2). He will be so ruthless and so domineering that no one will be able to stop him. Worse, many people all over the earth will be filled with great admiration for him. They will worship him, saying, "Who is like the beast? Who is able to make war with him?" (verse 4).

With great power, Antiochus IV controlled and persecuted the Jews. And with satanic hatred, the Antichrist will kill the Jews (Matthew 24:15-21) and the tribulation saints (Daniel 7:25; Revelation 13:7). No one will be able to resist him because "authority [will be] given him over every tribe, tongue, and nation."

Yet while the Antichrist's authority will be great, it will also be limited by God. Just as God permitted Satan to do only so much against Job (Job 2:6), the Antichrist will be given permission to do only so much against the Jewish people and those who follow Christ.

After these revelations were given to Daniel, the prophet was told to "seal up the vision, for it refers to many days in the future" (Daniel 8:26). Much of what was written in Daniel would not make sense until Earth's last days. What the book of Daniel seals, the book of Revelation unseals. In fact, the apostle John was told, "Do not seal the words of the prophecy of this book, for the time is at hand" (Revelation 22:10).

As we close this chapter and move to the next, we are reminded that the God of heaven alone is in control of the affairs of mankind. King Nebuchadnezzar came and went. The kingdoms of Medo-Persia, Greece, and Rome have come and gone. But the kingdom of God will endure and is eternal.

PROMISES MADE, PROMISES KEPT

DANIEL 9:1-19

What made Daniel such an outstanding servant of the Lord?

As we've made our way through the book of Daniel, we've seen this prophet's incredible character on display. He was uncompromising, gracious, and bold. He exhibited great wisdom as well as genuine humility. He spoke with integrity and gave God the credit for his accomplishments. He remained pure and undefiled in a pagan society governed by corrupt authorities. He sought to please God, not men. Kings knew they could trust him to tell the truth. In these ways and more, we see Daniel as a man of extraordinary faith.

In the opening verses of Daniel chapter 9, we find Daniel engaged in two activities that surely contributed to making him the person he was.

First, in verse 2, we find Daniel in "the books." Here, we're given a glimpse of the prophet as a diligent student of God's Word. At the moment, he was reading the words of Jeremiah. We can tell he was deeply stirred by what he read because it burdened his heart and prompted him to prayer. He also put on sackcloth and ashes and fasted. These are the actions of someone who pays such close attention to Scripture that he is highly responsive to it. Daniel was serious about the discipline of reading God's Word and letting it shape his life.

Second, we read that Daniel set his face "toward the Lord God to make request by prayer and supplications" (verse 3). Earlier, we saw that Daniel was so dedicated to prayer he was willing to be thrown into the lions' den. He prayed even when he knew that doing so could lead to his death. Daniel was serious about the discipline of prayer.

A person who is devoted to understanding the Scriptures and seeking God in prayer is a vessel ready for the Master's use. The more we are yielded to God, the more He can do through us. Daniel eagerly pursued God, and God did the rest. Surely, Daniel's zeal for Scripture and prayer prepared him to be used in mighty ways by God. May we learn from his example!

CAPTURE THE SCENE (What do I see?)

Using your Bible, answer the following questions.

1. What did Daniel discover while he was reading the prophet Jeremiah (Daniel 9:2)?

2. What actions did this discovery prompt Daniel to take (verse 3)?

3. What major theme runs all through Daniel's prayer (see verses 5, 8, 10-11)?

4. What specific pleas does Daniel set before the Lord in...

    a. verse 16?—

    b. verse 17?—

    c. verse 18?—

    d. verse 19?—

ANALYZE THE MESSAGE (What does it say and mean?)

Using both your Bible and your copy of the book *Discovering Daniel*, answer the following questions.

1. Daniel 9:2 tells us the prophet was reading the book of Jeremiah when he noticed a prophecy about the length of Judah's exile in Babylon.

    a. What passage had Daniel read in the book of Jeremiah (see page 171 in *Discovering Daniel*)?

b. What promise did God give in this prophecy (see page 171 in *Discovering Daniel*)?

c. What was the near-term fulfillment of this prophecy, and the far-term fulfillment (see page 171 in *Discovering Daniel*)?

2. In Daniel 9:3, what clues are we given about the intensity of Daniel's prayer?

3. As you read through the prayer, observe the many times that Daniel used the words *we*, *us*, and *our*. Though Daniel was a righteous man, he included himself in this prayer of repentance along with the rest of the people of Judah.

a. Why do you think Daniel included himself in the request for God's forgiveness (see page 177 in *Discovering Daniel*)?

b. Do you see a parallel here with Paul calling himself the chief of sinners in 1 Timothy 1:15? Explain.

4. In verse 18, Daniel said, "We do not present our supplications before You because of our righteous deeds, but because of Your great mercies." Daniel had a correct understanding of people's inability to be righteous and their need for God's mercy. What do the following passages say about our deeds versus God's mercy?

a. Romans 5:8—

b. Ephesians 2:4-5—

c. Ephesians 2:8-9—

d. Titus 3:5—

COMPARE THIS PASSAGE WITH THE REST OF SCRIPTURE
(How is it supported elsewhere in the Bible?)

1. In Deuteronomy 28:15-68, God warned the people of Israel about the high cost of disobedience. He began by saying, "It shall come to pass, if you do not obey the voice of the LORD your God, to observe carefully all His commandments and statutes which I command you today, that all these curses will come upon you and overtake you."

    God then listed the curses the people would experience. Look up the verses below. What specific punishments line up with the fallout that occurred when the Babylonians conquered Jerusalem and took Hebrew captives into exile?

    a. Verse 20—

    b. Verse 25—

    c. Verse 32—

    d. Verse 36—

e. Verses 48-49—

f. Verse 52—

2. At the same time Jeremiah warned of judgment, he also offered hope. God's promise in Jeremiah 29:10 caught Daniel's attention: "When seventy years are completed for Babylon, I will visit you, and I will fulfill to you my promise and bring you back to this place."

Daniel knew with certainty that God keeps His promises. He knew it was time for the people of Judah to get ready for the day when God would allow them to return to their homeland. What's interesting is that God said He would fulfill this promise regardless of the spiritual state of His people.

Even so, Daniel saw the need for the people to repent. God was ready to follow through on His commitment. Daniel's desire was for the people to follow through on their obligation to God. He wanted them to have a change of heart and obey God again.

a. What assurances are we given about God's promises in the following passages?

1) Numbers 23:19—

2) 1 Kings 8:56—

b. A major focal point of Daniel's prayer was the confession of sin. What do we learn about confession in the verses below?

1) Psalm 32:2-5—

2) Psalm 51:4—

3) Proverbs 28:13—

4) 1 John 1:9—

EXECUTE (How does this affect my life?)

1. Daniel's dedication to understanding Scripture and his devotion to praying fervently made for a powerful combination. Have you ever considered that to carry out one of those habits without the other can be detrimental? Ask yourself:

   a. What are the potential dangers of being a good student of God's Word but negligent in prayer?

   b. What are the potential dangers of being fervent in prayer without having a clear understanding of Scripture?

2. Scripture makes it clear that God takes sin seriously. The question is, Do we take sin seriously enough? As you consider your perspective of sin, answer the questions below:

   a. What effect did the sin of eating from a specific tree have on the entire human race (see Romans 5:12)?

   b. What effect does sin have on us (Isaiah 59:2)?

c. What did Christ do to make forgiveness possible for us (see Isaiah 53:5; 1 Peter 3:18)?

d. Read Galatians 5:16-18. Is it possible for us to walk in the Spirit and walk in sin at the same time? Explain.

e. In light of the above, why do you think God hates sin so much?

f. Why is it dangerous for us to downplay the seriousness of sin?

3. According to Hebrews 4:12, what resource has God given us to help examine our hearts and see whether we are allowing sin to reside within us? What does this tell us about the priority this resource should have in our lives?

CLOSING THOUGHTS

Daniel realized that the 70 years of captivity were almost up. And his people would soon be able to return to Jerusalem. But what would they find there?

Who was now occupying what was left of their houses, farms, and lands? An entire generation of Hebrews had been born and died off, having never seen the land of God's promise. And any person who was alive at the time Judah was taken into exile would be in his or her eighties or older.

Between the destruction of their homeland and 70 years of exile in Babylon, the people of Judah had been through a lot. They may have wondered, along with the psalmist:

> Will the Lord cast off forever?
> And will He be favorable no more?
> Has His mercy ceased forever?
> Has His promise failed forevermore?
> Has God forgotten to be gracious?
> Has He in anger shut up His tender mercies? (Psalm 77:7-9).

But then the psalmist realized that instead of looking down at his circumstances, he should look up to God's faithfulness. It's when we remember God's track record of keeping His promises that our fears are replaced with hope:

> I said, "This is my anguish;
> but I will remember the years of the right hand of the Most High."
> I will remember the works of the LORD;
> surely I will remember Your works of old.
> I will also meditate on all Your work,
> and talk of Your deeds.
> Your way, O God, is in the sanctuary;
> who is so great a God as our God?
> You are the God who does wonders;
> You have declared Your strength among the peoples.
> You have with Your arm redeemed Your people,
> the sons of Jacob and Joseph (verses 10-15).

Great is His faithfulness!

THE MESSIANIC COUNTDOWN

DANIEL 9:20-24

One day when Daniel was reading the words of the prophet Jeremiah, he came across God's promise that the Babylonian captivity would last 70 years. After that, the people of Judah would be free to return home. This caught Daniel's attention, for he knew the 70-year sentence was almost up. And he knew that God is a God who keeps His promises.

First, Daniel and his fellow Hebrews had seen God stay true to His warning that their disobedience would result in captivity. In Deuteronomy 28, God had said that if His people failed to observe His commandments, they would be punished. They persisted in their rebellion, and God was patient. But a point came when their sin had worn Him down. In 722 BC, the northern kingdom of Israel was taken captive by Assyria. Then from 605 BC to 586 BC, in three successive waves, King Nebuchadnezzar's armies conquered the southern kingdom of Judah and took many exiles to faraway Babylon.

Second, God had said the captivity would last for 70 years (Jeremiah 25:11). Daniel knew that as surely as God had fulfilled His promises to punish the people, He would sovereignly work out the details so they could return home. God had given the land to them as an everlasting possession, and He would bring them back. Why? Because of His love for them: "After seventy years are completed at Babylon, I will visit you and perform My good word toward you, and cause you to return to this place. For I know the thoughts that I think toward you…thoughts of peace and not of evil, to give you a future and a hope" (29:10-11).

God gave a third promise on the heels of the second one: "It will come to pass, when seventy years are completed, that I will punish the king of Babylon and that nation, the land of the Chaldeans, for their iniquity." Though God had used the Babylonians to chastise His people, He would avenge them for how they had treated the exiles from Judah. He would "repay [the Babylonians] according to the works of their own hands" (Jeremiah 25:14).

As Daniel pondered these prophetic promises, he desired greater understanding: "I set my face toward the Lord God to make request by prayer and supplications" (Daniel 9:3).

When we reach the end of the prophet's prayer, Daniel chapter 9 takes a totally unexpected turn. God's answer to this beloved servant was far more than what was expected. In Daniel's search for clarity about prophecies with *near* fulfillments, God revealed some mind-blowing prophecies with *distant* fulfillments—prophecies about the Messiah's arrival on Earth, and about Israel's future.

All given with the most amazing mathematical precision.

CAPTURE THE SCENE (What do I see?)

Using your Bible, answer the following questions.

1. What happened while Daniel was praying (see Daniel 9:20-21)?

2. What was the purpose of Daniel's visitor (see verse 22)?

3. What special sentiment does this visitor communicate to Daniel (see verse 23)?

4. Read Daniel 9:24.

   a. What time span does this prophecy cover?

   b. Whose people and which city is this prophecy for?

   c. What does this prophecy say will be accomplished?

ANALYZE THE MESSAGE (What does it say and mean?)

Using both your Bible and your copy of the book *Discovering Daniel*, answer the following questions.

1. Do we ever need to wonder whether God is hearing our prayers, and why (see page 187 in *Discovering Daniel*)?

2. What four words in 1 John 5:14 define how we are to pray (see page 188 in *Discovering Daniel*)?

3. What is the best way for us to understand the Hebrew word translated "weeks" in Daniel 9:24 (see pages 189-190 in *Discovering Daniel*)?

4. With that in mind, what period of time was Gabriel referring to (see page 190 in *Discovering Daniel*)?

5. What four divisions do we see within the 70 weeks (see pages 190-191 in *Discovering Daniel*)?

6. List the six purposes or goals that were to be accomplished through this 70-weeks prophecy (Daniel 9:24; see page 191 in *Discovering Daniel*—note that each one of these purposes or goals begins with the word *to*)?

7. What do the first three purposes have in common (see pages 192-195 in *Discovering Daniel*)?

8. In Daniel 9:24, the first purpose of Jesus' second coming is "to bring in everlasting righteousness." When will this happen, and what Scripture passage supports this (see pages 196-197 in *Discovering Daniel*)?

9. The next purpose of Jesus' second coming is "to seal up vision and prophecy." Does this mean there are no more prophecies that will need fulfillment? Explain (see page 197 in *Discovering Daniel*).

10. In Daniel 9:24, the phrase "Most Holy" likely refers to the fourth temple. Why does it make sense to conclude it's about the *fourth* temple and not the *third* (see page 199 in *Discovering Daniel*)?

COMPARE THIS PASSAGE WITH THE REST OF SCRIPTURE
(How is it supported elsewhere in the Bible?)

When we look at the purposes of Christ's first and second comings, ultimately, they can be broken down into three parts: the problem, the solution, and the reign.

1. *The Problem:* What do the following passages say is the dilemma of every human on Earth?

   a. Romans 3:10-11—

   b. Romans 3:23—

   c. Ephesians 2:1-3—

2. ***The Solution:*** According to the verses below, what is the one and only answer to every person's greatest need?

a. John 3:16—

b. 2 Corinthians 5:21—

c. 1 Peter 2:24—

3. ***The Reign:*** What promised renewal can we look forward to?

a. Isaiah 2:2-4—

b. Jeremiah 23:5-6—

c. Daniel 7:13-14—

EXECUTE (How does this affect my life?)

1. Daniel received an immediate answer to his prayer. That can happen to us as well. But there are also times when the Lord says *no* or *wait*. Consider the following:

   a. *When the Lord Says No*

      1) Read 2 Corinthians 12:7-10. When the apostle Paul asked God to remove "a thorn in the flesh," what did God say?

      2) What was Paul's attitude when God said no, and why?

      3) Can you think of two or three reasons God might say no to a prayer request?

   b. *When the Lord Says Wait*

      1) When Lazarus was seriously ill, his sisters Mary and Martha sent for Jesus. But Jesus did not visit them right away. In the meantime,

Lazarus died. What does the last part of John 11:4 give as the reason for Jesus' delay?

2) What are two or three other reasons God might delay an answer to prayer?

3) Can you think of a time in your own life when a delayed answer turned out to be the best answer?

2. As we continue into the next lesson, we'll learn more about the 70-weeks prophecy. But already, we're getting a clear picture of how precisely God had planned out the rest of history from Daniel's day all the way to the millennial kingdom—a span of thousands of years that involves an amazing number of moving parts that have to be perfectly orchestrated in order for God's plans to be fulfilled.

a. What does this tell you about God?

b. How should this influence the way you live?

c. How should this affect any fears or concerns you have about the future?

CLOSING THOUGHTS

When Daniel prayed in response to Jeremiah's prophecy about the end of the Babylonian captivity, the answer he received was a lot more than he expected. God was pleased to reveal not only the near future, but the distant future as well.

Repeatedly through the book of Daniel, we see God reveal details about human history all the way from the days of the Babylonian kingdom to the end times and beyond. Much of what was prophesied in Daniel is now in the past—and it was fulfilled with stunning precision. This gives us confidence that the prophecies about the future will similarly come to pass as well.

Fulfilled prophecy is a powerful testimony to the accuracy of Scripture. It is confirmation that the Bible is of divine origin and can be trusted. No mere human could possibly predict the future so perfectly. Only God possesses the ability to foresee what is to come and to sovereignly bring it about.

As 2 Peter 1:19-21 says:

> We have the prophetic word confirmed, which you do well to heed as a light that shines in a dark place, until the day dawns and the morning star rises in your hearts; knowing this first, that no prophecy of Scripture is of any private interpretation, for prophecy never came by the will of man, but holy men of God spoke as they were moved by the Holy Spirit.

SEVENTY WEEKS ALL ACCOUNTED FOR

DANIEL 9:25-27

If there is one lesson we can learn from Bible prophecy, it is this: God's Word always comes to pass.

That alone is remarkable. Especially when we consider that there are many hundreds of prophecies in Scripture, including some that are quite detailed.

But Daniel 9:24-27 takes all this up to another level of awesome.

Admittedly, the math here gets complicated. It takes a bit of work to figure out. But there are some who have rolled up their sleeves and crunched the numbers, and they check out. Not vaguely, but specifically—to the day.

At first glance, the numbers might seem just that—numbers. But they inform us of the orderly way God has planned the history and future of both the Jewish people and Gentiles. He has well-defined purposes in mind.

From the time King Artaxerxes commissioned Nehemiah to rebuild the city to the day Jesus rode into Jerusalem comes to 173,880 days, or 483 years. That's the time frame the angel Gabriel gave to Daniel—a time that is part of God's master plan for Israel.

This corresponds to the first 69 weeks of Daniel's 70-week prophecy.

Then God's time clock would pause for an unknown length of time for what we now call the church age.

But there is still one week left on God's time clock—the seventieth week.

This corresponds to the future seven-year tribulation, which will end at the exact time God has preordained. Christ will return right on time.

No one here on Earth has had to orchestrate people and events to ensure all this would play out as God planned. God alone has done and continues to do all the work. He didn't have to ask for cooperation from anyone.

Even if we find ourselves still feeling a bit confused after going through the numbers of weeks laid out in Daniel 9:24-27, the most important truth in this passage is abundantly clear and easy to grasp.

God is in control.

CAPTURE THE SCENE (What do I see?)

Using your Bible, answer the following questions. So that you can more easily understand the time references in Daniel 9:25-27, remember that "weeks" refers to weeks of *years*.

If you feel uncertain about some of the answers, leave them blank, and continue onward through the **Analyze the Message** section. After you've completed that, you might try coming back to the items you've left blank in **Capture the Scene** and see if you've gained additional knowledge that can help fill in those blanks.

1. According to verse 25, what event will mark the *beginning* of the first "seven weeks and sixty-two weeks" of this prophecy?

2. What does verse 25 say will be built again?

3. Who will be "cut off" after the 62 weeks (verse 26)?

4. In the middle of verse 26, we read about a certain group of people who will come. What will these people do, according to the last part of verse 26?

5. According to verse 27, what will be confirmed, and for how long?

6. What will happen at the middle of that week (or period of seven years)?

7. When the last part of verse 27 talks about "one who makes desolate," what does that seem to suggest?

8. Daniel 9:27 says this will happen "until the consummation, which is determined." What do you think the fact this "is determined" suggests?

ANALYZE THE MESSAGE (What does it say and mean?)

Using both your Bible and your copy of the book *Discovering Daniel*, answer the following questions.

1. What good news did Gabriel first share about Jerusalem in Daniel 9:25 (see page 202 in *Discovering Daniel*)?

2. What bad news did Gabriel then share in verse 26 (see page 208 in *Discovering Daniel*)?

3. What kind of Messiah were the Jews looking for (see page 208 in *Discovering Daniel*)?

4. What kind of Messiah did they get instead (see pages 208-209 in *Discovering Daniel*)?

5. A point came when the Jewish leaders were hostile and the people were disillusioned. What did they demand be done to the Messiah (see page 209 in *Discovering Daniel*)?

6. Read Isaiah 53:4-6 on pages 209-210 of *Discovering Daniel*. What comes to your mind as you read this description of what happened at the cross?

7. On page 211 of *Discovering Daniel*, we read that "looking forward to the fulfillment of prophecy is like looking at a mountain range." What is meant by this?

8. Who is the person identified as "he" in verse 27, and what does the fact there is sacrifice going on tell us (see page 212 in *Discovering Daniel*)?

9. How do we know from the Hebrew text of verse 27 that the covenant mentioned here is no ordinary covenant? And what might make this covenant so momentous (see page 212 in *Discovering Daniel*)?

10. What is the significance of the Antichrist bringing "an end to sacrifice and offering" (verse 27)? How will the Antichrist profane the temple (see page 213 in *Discovering Daniel*)?

11. Read Matthew 24:15-18. What did Jesus warn the Jewish people to do when they saw the "abomination of desolation" (see also page 213 in *Discovering Daniel*)?

COMPARE THIS PASSAGE WITH THE REST OF SCRIPTURE
(How is it supported elsewhere in the Bible?)

When God carries out His work, He is never too early or too late. Consider the following, in relation to Jesus:

1. According to Galatians 4:4, when did God send forth His Son?

2. When Lazarus was ill, his sisters Mary and Martha sent for Jesus, who did not come right away. Lazarus ended up dying before Jesus arrived.

   a. What assumption did Martha make in John 11:21?

   b. In verse 32, what did Mary assume?

   c. In verse 37, what question did some of the crowd ask?

d. In words spoken to the Father, what reason did Jesus give for waiting until Lazarus died before doing anything?

e. What does this tell you about Jesus' timing?

3. In Zechariah 9:9, we read a prophecy about Israel's King entering Jerusalem on "a colt, the foal of a donkey." Now read carefully about the fulfillment of this prophecy (hundreds of years later) in Matthew 21:1-9. Do you think that when Jesus commanded two of His disciples to find and bring the colt of a donkey, that this was merely a random event? Why or why not?

4. Jesus' entrance into Jerusalem—and His being "cut off" through the crucifixion—is foreseen in Daniel 9:26, a passage that lays out God's prophetic timetable with amazing mathematical precision. What affect does this have on how you view Christ, and how you view Bible prophecy?

EXECUTE (How does this affect my life?)

God sent forth His Son "when the fullness of time had come" (Galatians 4:4). That is, at exactly the right time. Every prophecy that Jesus fulfilled during His first coming came to pass right on schedule. Remarkably, this aspect of God's sovereignty isn't limited to the work He did and continues to do through Jesus, as you'll see in the passages below.

1. Where does Psalm 31:15 say that our times are?

2. In Psalm 139:16, we read,

> Your eyes saw my substance, being yet unformed.
> And in Your book they all were written,
> the days fashioned for me,
> when as yet there were none of them.

   What does this passage tell us God has done with the days of our lives?

3. Read Luke 12:6-7. How detailed is God's knowledge of us?

4. Based on the above passages, how much do you think God is involved in your life? How does that encourage you?

5. As Psalm 139:16 says, God wrote out your days before you were born. With that in mind, do you feel you are making the best use of the time God has entrusted to you? In what two or three areas do you see room for growth or improvement?

CLOSING THOUGHTS

God's divine intervention in people's lives is on display all through the Bible. We've seen this all through the book of Daniel. In the New Testament, one particularly stunning example of this is found in John 19, during Jesus' encounter with Pilate.

As the crowds were pressuring Pilate to have Jesus crucified, Pilate asked Him, "Where are You from?" (verse 9). Jesus gave no answer. This frustrated Pilate. He said,

> "Are you not speaking to me? Do You not know that I have power to crucify You, and power to release You?"

> Jesus answered, "You could have no power at all against Me unless it had been given you from above" (verses 10-11).

Pilate's power "had been given...*from above*"!

The Roman governor was frightened. "From then on Pilate sought to release

Him" (verse 12). But the crowds wouldn't have it: "If you let this man go, you are not Caesar's friend. Whoever makes himself a king speaks against Caesar."

In the end, Pilate used the authority vested in him—*from above*—to deliver Jesus to be crucified.

It is sobering to consider God's sovereignty over every person's life, including our own. But the same sovereignty that reminds us of our great accountability to God also evidences His great love for us. We can count on Him to use His sovereignty not only to motivate us to obedience, but also to watch over us, protect us, and guide us in the way He would want us to go.

THE UNSEEN WARFARE

DANIEL 10

Satan does not care for Bible prophecy.

He doesn't want people to know what God will do in the future. There are a number of reasons for that. But the biggest one is this: Prophecy shows that in the end, God wins, and Satan loses. Badly.

In Daniel 10, we see Satan's effort to suppress prophecy on a grand scale. He didn't want God's messenger to reach Daniel and reveal what would happen in the latter days. Satan prefers that people be kept in the dark. He doesn't want them to see beyond the present chaos. Bible prophecy encourages people to look up to God and enables them to see the future with clarity. And that, in turn, gives them hope.

Which is why we can be sure the adversary is delighted when God's people are ignorant about Bible prophecy. He is pleased when churches and seminaries don't teach it. He breathes a sigh of relief when Christians give up on studying prophecy because they think it's too complicated to understand.

But God was intentional about including prophecies in the Bible. They are there for reasons that are good for us. Chief among them is so that we would know about Christ's first and second comings. God wanted us to know He would send a Savior who would deliver us from sin and bring us back to Him. And that this same Savior would later return to destroy His enemies, set up His kingdom, and rule the earth.

The prophet Daniel experienced firsthand the fierce opposition Satan had to prophecy. Let's dig in and learn more about the unseen warfare that affected Daniel—and continues to affect us today.

CAPTURE THE SCENE (What do I see?)

Using your Bible, answer the following questions.

1. Read Daniel 10:1-3. What happened to Daniel, and how did he respond?

2. What clues do you see in verses 1-3 that spiritual warfare was taking place?

3. What did Daniel see when he stood by the Tigris River (see verses 4-6)?

4. How did Daniel's companions respond (see verse 7)?

5. What happened to Daniel physically in response to this vision (see verses 8-9)?

6. Read verses 10-11.

   a. What did the visitor do to Daniel?

   b. What endearing words did this visitor say to Daniel?

7. According to verse 12, when did this visitor begin his journey to respond to Daniel?

8. How long did it take for this visitor to reach Daniel, and why (see verse 13)?

9. What was the visitor's reason for coming to Daniel (see verse 14)?

10. What was Daniel's emotional and physical response at this point (see verses 15-17)?

11. What encouragement did the visitor give Daniel (see verse 18)?

12. For what reason did the visitor say, "I must return" (see verse 20)?

ANALYZE THE MESSAGE (What does it say and mean?)

Using both your Bible and your copy of the book *Discovering Daniel*, answer the following questions.

1. How do we account for all the chaos, hatred, and misery in the world (see page 216 in *Discovering Daniel*)?

2. What does Satan's army of minions do (see page 217 in *Discovering Daniel*)?

3. Where do the battles between good and evil take place, and what effects do these skirmishes have (see pages 217-218 in *Discovering Daniel*)?

4. How do the ESV and NIV more accurately translate Daniel 10:1 (see page 219 in *Discovering Daniel*), and why do you think this distinction is significant?

5. What does the fact Daniel was called "man greatly beloved" tell you about how the Lord viewed Daniel (see page 222 in *Discovering Daniel*)? Why do you think this is important with regard to God revealing this and other visions to Daniel?

6. James 5:16—"The effective, fervent prayer of a righteous man avails much"—tells us of the cause and effect of prayer. In Daniel 10:12, the messenger said to the prophet, "I have come because of your words." When it comes to our own prayers, why do you think it is helpful for us to keep this cause and effect in mind?

7. List some of the reasons given for delayed answers to prayer, according to pages 224-225 of *Discovering Daniel.*

8. God sent a messenger in response to Daniel's prayer, but the messenger was delayed by "the prince of the kingdom of Persia" (Daniel 10:13). This prince of Persia evidently did not want Daniel to receive an answer to his prayer. What thoughts come to your mind as you consider the existence of the very real world of unseen spiritual warfare?

COMPARE THIS PASSAGE WITH THE REST OF SCRIPTURE
(How is it supported elsewhere in the Bible?)

1. Read Daniel 10:5-6 and compare it with Revelation 1:12-16. What similarities do you see between the two passages? (This serves as affirmation that Daniel saw a Christophany, or a preincarnate appearance of the Son of God.)

2. In Daniel 10:11, the prophet was told he was a "man greatly beloved." What similar affirmations do we see given to...

   a. Abraham in Isaiah 41:8?—

   b. David in 1 Samuel 13:14?—

   c. Mary in Luke 1:28?—

   d. John in John 21:7?—

3. In Daniel 10, the curtain is pulled back and we're given a glimpse of how a demonic spirit attempts to prevent Daniel from receiving an answer to his prayer. This is the way Satan has operated since the beginning, in the Garden of Eden. He does all he can to hinder God's communication to His own or to cause them to misunderstand God. How do we see this manifest in Matthew 16:21-23?

EXECUTE (How does this affect my life?)

1. What do you think are some of the reasons Daniel was called "man greatly beloved" in Daniel 10:11? List them here. Which one or two of these characteristics would you like to strengthen in your own life? What are some ways you can make growth happen?

2. On page 226 of *Discovering Daniel*, we read that "there are demonic spirits today that do not want anyone to know God's plan for Israel, the church, or the nations." In what ways do we make ourselves spiritually vulnerable when we're ignorant of what God teaches us in Scripture?

3. Spiritual warfare is a constant in the Christian life. Why do you think prayer is such a vital tool for us when we face spiritual battles?

4. Daniel was deeply burdened by what God revealed to him. Can you think of a recent example of a time when a specific Bible passage weighed heavily on your heart? What passage was it, and what do you believe God was trying to teach you?

CLOSING THOUGHTS

Spiritual warfare is real. Satan is determined to defeat us. Though he can never take away our salvation, and he can never separate us from Christ's love, he will do all he can to discourage us, impede our spiritual growth, or lure us into sin through various kinds of temptations. His attacks against us will be relentless.

First Peter 5:8 urges us, "Be sober, be vigilant; because your adversary the devil walks about like a roaring lion, seeking whom he may devour." This is why 1 Peter 1:13 calls us to "gird up the loins of your mind, be sober." We're to be watchful and alert.

James 4:7 gives insight on the best first step we can take when it comes to spiritual battle: "Submit to God. Resist the devil and he will flee from you." *Submit to God.* Only then can we resist the devil. Here, to submit means being fully yielded. Our inclination is to cling to favorite "little sins" in the corners of our lives, and to think such sins aren't all that harmful to us. But to do this hurts us because it means we are less than wholly submitted to God.

All through the book of Daniel, we've seen the prophet characterized by an uncompromising life. As one fully submitted to God in all things, he is our example of what it takes to resist the influences of a secular culture and to stand strong in spiritual battle. At times, the intensity of the warfare overwhelmed Daniel and left him feeling worn out. This will happen to us as well. But Daniel did not surrender. He endured. And with God's enablement, so can we.

THE LONG JOURNEY TO THE ANTICHRIST

DANIEL 11

As we've made our way through Daniel, we've read about a number of different kings and kingdoms. Daniel 11 continues that pattern. Within the first two verses, we come across five kings. Keeping track of so much history can be a challenge, but there are reasons God includes these details in His Word. One is to demonstrate His foreknowledge of the future—Bible prophecy is history written in advance. Another reason is to confirm His sovereignty. It is God who "changes the times and the seasons; He removes kings and raises up kings" (Daniel 2:21). It is He who "determined their preappointed times and the boundaries of their dwellings" (Acts 17:26). The destinies of rulers and nations are in His hands.

Daniel 11 reveals to us that God will continue to steer the direction of history all the way to the time of the world's final empire—that of the Antichrist. We are introduced to this extraordinarily wicked ruler in verse 36: He "shall do according to his own will: he shall exalt and magnify himself above every god, shall speak blasphemies against the God of gods, and shall prosper till the wrath has been accomplished; for what has been determined shall be done."

Did you catch the part about "till the wrath has been accomplished"?

God has placed a time limit on the Antichrist's reign. When the tribulation runs its course, the Antichrist will meet his end. He and his kingdom will be utterly crushed when the King of kings and Lord of lords returns to set up His eternal kingdom. Every human king and kingdom will become as nothing, relics on the ash heap of history.

Daniel 11 takes us on a tour through kingdoms in defiance of God, and reveals they are all destined for defeat. The chapter is a triumphant testimony to the absolute sovereignty of God over all human affairs. No one can defy God and get away with it. For this reason, we can be confident about the future.

CAPTURE THE SCENE (What do I see?)

Using your Bible, answer the following questions. For now, we won't specify the names of the kingdoms behind these passages. Do your best to follow the action, and keep in mind that what we're seeing here is the constant rise and fall of human empires.

1. Who is the first king mentioned in Daniel 11 (see verse 1)? What are we told about the "mighty king" in verse 3? What will happen to this king's kingdom, according to verse 4?

2. In verse 5, what are we told about "the king of the South"? What will this king do, according to verses 7-8?

3. What will then take place between the kings of the North and South (see verses 11-13)?

4. What then happens in verses 14-16?

5. As you read verses 17-20, what words and phrases stand out to you as describing the arrogance of rulers and the chaos of human history?

6. In verse 21, we come to Antiochus Epiphanes IV. What are we told about his character?

7. In the grand sweep of all that we're told about Antiochus IV in verses 22-35, what words or phrases help to explain why this evil man is considered a foreshadow of the Antichrist?

8. In verse 36, we are introduced to the Antichrist. What is revealed about his character in verses 36-39?

9. In verses 40-45, we read of conquests, victories, and defeats. According to verse 45, how will it all end for the Antichrist?

ANALYZE THE MESSAGE (What does it say and mean?)

Using both your Bible and your copy of the book *Discovering Daniel*, answer the following questions.

1. In Daniel 11:1, we read that Daniel's messenger "stood up to confirm and strengthen him." When it comes to identifying who "him" is, what are the two options (see page 235 in *Discovering Daniel*)?

2. Even though we cannot be absolutely certain about the identity of "him," what can we be certain about (see page 235 in *Discovering Daniel*)?

3. Verses 3-4 talk about Alexander the Great. What ended up happening to his kingdom after his death (see page 237 in *Discovering Daniel*)?

4. In verses 5-20, we see a lot of back and forth take place through battles, attempts at alliances, and intrigue and deceit. Remember, all of this was written well before it ever happened.

   a. What is God telling us about Himself by giving all these details?

   b. What do we learn about humanity in these same details?

5. How did Antiochus IV become ruler, and what was the relationship between him and the Jews like, and why (see pages 243-244 in *Discovering Daniel*)?

6. What happened to Antiochus IV when he went to Egypt (see pages 244-245 in *Discovering Daniel*)?

7. In what specific ways did Antiochus IV unleash his anger upon the Jews, according to Daniel 11:31 (see page 245 in *Discovering Daniel*)?

8. What two different ways did the Jews respond to Antiochus IV (see pages 245-246 in *Discovering Daniel*)?

9. What was involved when Antiochus IV committed the "abomination of desolation" (see page 247 in *Discovering Daniel*)?

10. Read both Daniel 11:36-39 and 2 Thessalonians 2:9-12. Based on these descriptions, in what ways will the Antichrist be the complete opposite of the one true Christ?

11. According to Revelation 19:19-21, how will it all end for the Antichrist and his forces?

COMPARE THIS PASSAGE WITH THE REST OF SCRIPTURE
(How is it supported elsewhere in the Bible?)

All through Daniel chapter 11, we are repeatedly reminded of one sobering truth: Everything human is temporary. Nothing earthly will last. With that in mind, what wisdom do we glean from the following passages?

1. Matthew 10:28—

2. 2 Corinthians 4:17-18—

3. James 4:13-15—

4. 2 Peter 3:11—

EXECUTE (How does this affect my life?)

1. Based on what you read in Daniel 11, what did human rulers and their followers pursue and value most?

2. In the light of eternity, what perspective should we have about human achievements?

3. Read 1 Corinthians 3:12-15, which speaks of when believers will come before the judgment seat of Christ. Here, we read about our Lord's evaluation of our works done on Earth. As you answer the following two questions, don't come away with the impression that only "ministry service" counts toward good done for our Lord. It is possible for secular jobs, schooling, and everyday responsibilities to be done in ways that exalt God and accomplish His work—as 1 Corinthians 10:31 says, "Whatever you do, do all to the glory of God."

   a. Give two to four examples of motives and pursuits you would say can be described as gold, silver, and precious stones.

b. Give two to four examples of attitudes and achievements you think will be considered wood, hay, and straw.

4. Colossians 3:2 exhorts us, "Set your minds on things that are above, not on things that are on earth." Yet we will always find ourselves lured by the glitter of the temporary. What can we do to grow in our heavenly mindedness?

5. Based on what you read in Daniel 11, on the left side of the space below, write a list of the characteristics of earthly kings and kingdoms. Then on the right side of the space below, list the characteristics that you know will be true about Christ and His kingdom. What contrasts do you see?

CLOSING THOUGHTS

When the Antichrist comes on the world scene, he will captivate people with charm and deceit. He will rise to power quickly, and his arrogance, paired with Satan's power, will lead him to become the most blasphemous world leader of all time. Daniel 11 portrays him as one who will do whatever he wishes (verse 36). He will exalt himself above not only earthly gods but the one true God (verse 36).

The Antichrist will prosper at all he does, and nothing will stand in his way (verse 36). He will be hostile to religion and normal human affections (verse 37). He will place his confidence in his personal power and military might (verses 38-39), and he will know great success in battle (verses 40-43).

So great will the Antichrist's power be that he appears unstoppable.

Yet Daniel 11:45 is clear about his fate, which will occur swiftly: "[The Antichrist] shall come to his end, and no one will help him." The most sinister and corrupt emperor of all time will meet instant defeat when Christ returns. Nothing will be able to spare him. He will have every earthly and satanic force at his disposal. And yet he and all who assist him will be wiped out completely.

The finality of the Antichrist's defeat is made clear in Revelation 20:10. After Christ conquers the Antichrist at the second coming, He will set up His 1,000-year reign on Earth. At the end of that kingdom, Satan will attempt one last insurrection against our Lord, and be defeated. When the devil is thrown into the lake of fire, we're told that the Antichrist and his prophet are still there—1,000 years after the second coming. And we're told that is where they will stay, "day and night forever and ever."

A FINAL MESSAGE OF HOPE

DANIEL 12

The tribulation will be a time of great suffering for the Jewish people. The prophet Jeremiah put it this way: "Alas! For that day is great, so that none is like it; and it is the time of Jacob's trouble, but he shall be saved out of it" (Jeremiah 30:7).

This verse tells us the *what* and *why* of the tribulation. God planned it for the sake of Jacob—whom He renamed Israel (Genesis 32:28). Note that this period is called "the time of *Jacob's* trouble," and not the time of the *church's* trouble. It is Israel that will experience God's chastisement during the tribulation, not the church. The body of Christ will be absent—it will be taken up to heaven in the rapture, prior to the tribulation. Nowhere in Revelation chapters 4 through 18 do we see the church present on Earth.

God's purpose for the tribulation will be to bring about the salvation of His people Israel. It is at the end of this seven-year period of wrath that "they will look on [Him] whom they pierced" (Zechariah 12:10), and "all Israel will be saved" (Romans 11:26).

Daniel chapter 12 opens by affirming that this "time of trouble" will result in Israel being "saved out of it." First, Daniel delivers the bad news: "There shall be a time of trouble, such as never was since there was a nation, even to that time" (verse 1). During the tribulation, the Jewish people will face unprecedented horrors. The persecution the Antichrist will unleash upon God's people will be unparalleled. So much so that Jesus warned that "those who are in Judea [should] flee to the mountains" (Matthew 24:16).

Then after Daniel gives the bad news, he turns to the good news: "At that time your people shall be delivered, every one who is found written in the book" (Daniel 12:1).

What book is Daniel talking about? And whose names are written in it? Those are among the questions we will answer as we go through Daniel chapter 12—a chapter that speaks of the hope that lies ahead for Israel after it has faced God's refining fire.

Yet the message Daniel gives here is not only for Israel, but for *all* the people on the earth. Ultimately, it asks this question of great consequence: Where will you spend eternity?

CAPTURE THE SCENE (What do I see?)

Using your Bible, answer the following questions.

1. Read Daniel 12:1.

   a. Who will stand up?

   b. What is the responsibility of this "great prince"?

   c. What kind of trouble will occur?

d. What will be the end result of this trouble?

2. What two destinies will people awaken to, according to Daniel 12:2?

3. What command is Daniel given in verse 4?

4. Describe the interaction that Daniel witnesses between the "two others" in verses 5-7.

5. What question does Daniel ask in verse 8?

6. What answer is Daniel given in verse 9?

7. What are we told about the wicked and the wise in verse 10?

8. What events are described in verse 11, and what length of time is given here?

9. What will happen to those who wait and make it to 1,335 days (see verse 12)?

10. What final words does the angel give to Daniel in verse 13?

ANALYZE THE MESSAGE (What does it say and mean?)

Using both your Bible and your copy of the book *Discovering Daniel,* answer the following questions.

1. What specific words in Daniel 12:1 inform us of what Israel will face during the tribulation? What additional information are we given in Zechariah 13:8-9, and given the Jewish population in today's world, what numbers of casualties and survivors can we expect (see pages 258-261 in *Discovering Daniel*)?

2. How long of a time gap occurs between Daniel 12:1 and 12:2 (see page 261 in *Discovering Daniel*)?

3. What kind of resurrection do we view in verse 2 (see pages 261-262 in *Discovering Daniel*)?

4. How is this resurrection described in...

    a. John 5:28-29?—

b. Revelation 20:12-15?—

5. On page 264 of *Discovering Daniel*, we read, "What we wake up to then at the resurrection is entirely based on our choice now." If you were to explain this truth to an unbeliever, what Scripture passages would you use to confirm that their decision about Jesus affects their eternal destiny?

6. Why was Daniel told to "shut up the words, and seal the book until the time of the end" (12:4; see pages 265-266 in *Discovering Daniel*)?

7. We know from careful study that the "time, times, and half a time" in Daniel 12:7 refers to the severe persecution of the Jews during the last half of the tribulation. This comes to 1,260 days. But then verses 11 and 12 extend that to 1,290 days and 1,335 days. What is one plausible explanation for these extra days (see page 272 in *Discovering Daniel*)?

8. What wonderful promises are given to Daniel in verse 13? In light of all that Daniel endured during his years in captivity, why do you think these promises would be especially precious to him?

COMPARE THIS PASSAGE WITH THE REST OF SCRIPTURE
(How is it supported elsewhere in the Bible?)

1. To better understand how God will use the tribulation to chasten and purge His people, read the following passages. What results can come from suffering and trials?

   a. Romans 5:3-4—

   b. James 1:2-4—

   c. Hebrews 12:11—

2. Daniel 12:2-3 affirms that every person's choice about their eternal destiny is made during this life, and cannot be changed.

a. What will believers rise to, according to 2 Corinthians 5:6-8?

b. What will unbelievers rise to, according to 2 Thessalonians 1:8-9?

c. What does Matthew 25:46 confirm about the duration of the afterlife for both believers and unbelievers?

EXECUTE (How does this affect my life?)

1. All through the book of Daniel, we're given an example for how we are to live as Christians. The prophet is a role model of how to be a positive influence and shine God's light into a dark and sinful world. As you consider what you learned about Daniel, what inspired you most?

2. In what ways has your study of Daniel already motivated you to change how you live?

3. In Daniel 12, we see that Daniel didn't always come away with a perfectly clear understanding of God's revelations about the future. How do you find this fact helpful for your own study of Bible prophecy?

4. The final command given to Daniel is "Go your way till the end" (Daniel 12:13). This is a call to endurance. Why is it so vital that we persevere to the end in the Christian life, and not let up?

CLOSING THOUGHTS

Though the book of Daniel was written more than 2,500 years ago, it is timeless. In fact, the closer we get to the tribulation, the more relevant it becomes. Those who read it during that seven-year period of wrath will understand it better than anyone else in history because they will witness—with their own eyes—the unfolding of the many prophecies Daniel records about the end times.

Daniel is timeless because God is unchanging and knows the future perfectly. God is just as sovereign today as He was when the Babylonian, Medo-Persian, Greek, and Roman empires rose and fell. And He will be in control of all that takes place in the future. Not even the Antichrist will prevail over God.

From where God sits on His throne, He can see all of history at once. More importantly, He *plans* history. Isaiah 46:10 says that God declares "the end from the beginning...My counsel shall stand, and I will accomplish all my purpose." Proverbs 19:21 tells us, "Many are the plans in the mind of a man, but it is the purpose of the LORD that will stand."

People can plan all they want, but nothing can derail what God has determined will happen. That truth shines brightly all through Daniel—a book filled with accounts about the rise and fall of the world's most powerful kingdoms. All were as wet clay in God's firm hands.

This should give us enormous comfort in a day when the world is spiraling out of control morally and spiritually. No matter how bad things get, the book of Daniel teaches us God has the final say over what happens.

We can also be encouraged by the fact that Daniel was an ordinary person who became extraordinary only because he was empowered by God. Because he had set himself apart as a vessel for God's use, the Lord was able to use him in mighty ways. That is true about all the great men and women of the Bible.

We may think we could never be like Daniel. But it was God who made Daniel what he was. Daniel yielded himself fully, and God did the rest.

Our realm of influence may be much smaller, but that doesn't matter to God. Rather, what counts is that we submit ourselves to His use. When that happens, God's power is able to be unleashed through us.

From our perspective, we may think our service to the Lord is trivial compared to what Daniel did. But it's not. God is pleased when we give Him full reign over our lives. When we allow Him to work through us, the results are significant. We might not think so, but He does.

Those are the two messages that run constantly all through Daniel: God is sovereign, and He can do amazing things through those who are fully yielded to Him.

When you place your complete trust in those truths, you will have learned what God desires to teach you through Daniel. And you will allow the book's timeless message to shape how you live.

When that happens, then you will hear the words spoken to Daniel: "Go your way till the end, for you shall rest, and will arise to your inheritance at the end of the days" (Daniel 12:13).

Amir Tsarfati, with Dr. Rick Yohn, examines what Revelation makes known about the end times and beyond. Guided by accessible teaching that lets Scripture speak for itself, you'll see what lies ahead for every person in the end times—either in heaven or on Earth. Are *you* ready?

This companion workbook to *Revealing Revelation*—the product of many years of careful research—offers you a clear and exciting overview of God's perfect plan for the future. Inside you'll find principles from the Bible that equip you to better interpret the end-times signs, as well as insights about how Bible prophecy is relevant to your life today.

In *Israel and the Church*, bestselling author and native Israeli Amir Tsarfati helps readers recognize the distinct contemporary and future roles of both the Jewish people and the church, and how together they reveal the character of God and His perfect plan of salvation.

To fully grasp what God has in store for the future, it's vital to understand His promises to Israel. The *Israel and the Church Study Guide* will help you do exactly that, equipping you to explore the Bible's many revelations about what is yet to come.

As a native Israeli of Jewish roots, Amir Tsarfati provides a distinct perspective that weaves biblical history, current events, and Bible prophecy together to shine light on the mysteries about the end times. In *The Day Approaching*, he points to the scriptural evidence that the return of the Lord is imminent.

Jesus Himself revealed the signs that will alert us to the nearness of His return. In *The Day Approaching Study Guide*, you'll have the opportunity to take an up-close look at what those signs are, as well as God's overarching plans for the future, and how those plans affect you today.

Bestselling author and native Israeli Amir Tsarfati provides clarity on what will happen during the tribulation and explains its place in God's timeline.

With this study guide companion to *Has the Tribulation Begun?*, bestselling author and prophecy expert Amir Tsarfati guides you through a biblical overview of the last days, with thought-provoking study and application questions.

In *Bible Prophecy: The Essentials*, Amir and Barry team up to answer 70 of their most commonly asked questions, which focus on seven foundational themes of Bible prophecy: Israel, the church, the rapture, the tribulation, the millennium, the Great White Throne judgment, and heaven.

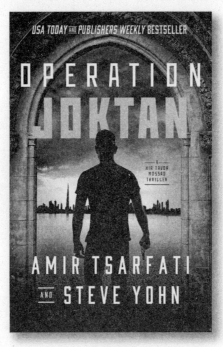

USA TODAY AND PUBLISHERS WEEKLY BESTSELLER

OPERATION JOKTAN

A NIR TAVOR MOSSAD THRILLER

AMIR TSARFATI AND STEVE YOHN

BOOK 1

"It was the perfect day—until the gunfire."

Nir Tavor is an Israeli secret service operative turned talented Mossad agent.

Nicole le Roux is a model with a hidden skill.

A terrorist attack brings them together, and then work forces them apart—until they're unexpectedly called back into each other's lives.

But there's no time for romance. As violent radicals threaten chaos across the Middle East, the two must work together to stop these extremists, pooling Nicole's knack for technology and Nir's adeptness with on-the-ground missions. Each heart-racing step of their operation gets them closer to the truth—and closer to danger.

In this thrilling first book in a new series, authors Amir Tsarfati and Steve Yohn draw on true events as well as tactical insights Amir learned from his time in the Israeli Defense Forces. For believers in God's life-changing promises, *Operation Joktan* is a suspense-filled page-turner that illuminates the blessing Israel is to the world.

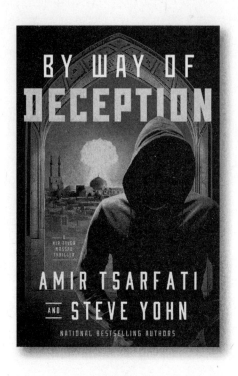

BOOK 2

The Mossad has uncovered Iran's plans to smuggle untraceable weapons of mass destruction into Israel. The clock is ticking, and agents Nir Tavor and Nicole le Roux can't act quickly enough.

Nir and Nicole find themselves caught in a whirlwind plot of assassinations, espionage, and undercover recon, fighting against the clock to stop this threat against the Middle East. As they draw closer to danger—and closer to each other—they find themselves ensnared in a lethal web of secrets. Will they have to sacrifice their own lives to protect the lives of millions?

Inspired by real events, authors Amir Tsarfati and Steve Yohn reteam for this suspenseful follow-up to the bestselling *Operation Joktan*. Filled with danger, romance, and international intrigue, this Nir Tavor thriller reveals breathtaking true insights into the lives and duties of Mossad agents—and delivers a story that will have you on the edge of your seat.

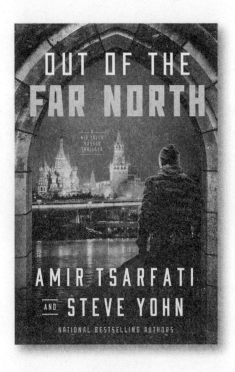

BOOK 3

Tensions are at a breaking point. The Western markets that once relied on Russian gas have turned to Israel for their energy needs. Furious, Russia moves to protect its interests by using its newfound ally, Iran, and Iran's proxy militias.

As Israel's elite fighting forces and the Mossad go undercover, they detect the Kremlin is planning a major attack against Israel. Hunting for clues, Mossad agents Nir Tavor and Nicole le Roux plunge themselves into the treacherous underworld of Russian oligarch money, power, and decadence.

With each danger they face, le Roux's newfound Christian faith grows stronger. And battle-weary Tavor—haunted by dreams from his past—must confront memories and pain he'd sought to bury.

In this electrifying thriller, hostilities explode as Tavor and le Roux fight to prevent a devastating conflict. Will they be able to outwit their enemies, or will their actions have catastrophic consequences?

BEHOLD ISRAEL

Behold Israel is a nonprofit organization founded and led by native Israeli Amir Tsarfati. Its mission is to provide reliable and accurate reporting on developments in Israel and the surrounding region.

Through Behold Israel's website, free app, social media, and teachings in multiple languages, the ministry reaches communities worldwide.

Amir's on-location teachings explain Israel's central role in the Bible and present the truth about current events amidst global media bias against Israel.

FOLLOW US ON SOCIAL

    @beholdisrael

BEHOLDISRAEL.ORG

To learn more about our Harvest Prophecy resources, please visit:

www.HarvestProphecyHQ.com

HARVEST PROPHECY
An Imprint of Harvest House Publishers